Little Red Book
of
Word Facts

Other Titles in the Series

Little Red Book of SMS Slang and Chat Room Slang	Little Red Book of Synonyms
Little Red Book of English Vocabulary Today	Little Red Book of Antonyms
	Little Red Book of Common Errors
Little Red Book of Grammar Made Easy	Little Red Book of Letter Writing
	Little Red Book of Essay Writing
Little Red Book of English Proverbs	Little Red Book of Spelling
	Little Red Book of Language Checklist
Little Red Book of Prepositions	
Little Red Book of Idioms and Phrases	Little Red Book of Perfect Written English
Little Red Book of Effective Speaking Skills	Little Red Book of Punctuation
	Little Red Book of Reading and Listening Skills
Little Red Book of Phrasal Verbs	
Little Red Book of Euphemisms	Little Red Book of A Child's First Dictionary
Little Red Book of Word Power	
Little Red Book of Modern Writing Skills	Little Red Book of Phonics

Little Red Book *of* Word Facts

Terry O'Brien

RUPA

Published by
Rupa Publications India Pvt. Ltd 2012
7/16, Ansari Road, Daryaganj
New Delhi 110002

Sales centres:
Prayagraj Bengaluru Chennai
Hyderabad Jaipur Kathmandu
Kolkata Mumbai

Copyright © Terry O'Brien 2012

All rights reserved.
No part of this publication may be reproduced, transmitted,
or stored in a retrieval system, in any form or by any means,
electronic, mechanical, photocopying, recording or otherwise,
without the prior permission of the publisher.

P-ISBN: 978-81-291-2106-6
E-ISBN: 978-81-291-3024-2

Sixth impression 2023

10 9 8 7 6

The moral right of the author has been asserted.

Typeset by Innovative Processors, New Delhi

Printed in India

This book is sold subject to the condition that it shall not, by way of trade
or otherwise, be lent, resold, hired out, or otherwise circulated, without
the publisher's prior consent, in any form of binding or cover other than
that in which it is published.

*I dedicate this book to late Prof. A.P. O'Brien,
my father, friend, guide and mentor, who
inspired me to the canon of excellence:
re-imagining what's essential*

PREFACE

Little Red Book of Word Facts is a book for all who love words. The book is a collection of fascinating facts about words. It deals with the nitty-gritty of common and not so common words in the English language.

The book is a result of my study of etymology and research on unusual words. The word trivia compiled here is for fun!

The book is aimed at being a catalyst for readers to begin the quest for interesting information on their own. It will also lead to clarity the differences between confusable words and how words are formed.

This book is an incomplete book. It is a beginning to explore further! It is time to read dictionaries also for fun.

> The letter **A** evolved from the Hebrew and Phoenician character *alep*, "ox"

Awhile means "for a time" and **a while** means "a period of time".

The lightest weight of sandpaper is **A** and the heaviest is **E**.

A-1 was originally an abbreviation in the Register of Shipping for Lloyds of London- used to describe ships in first-Class condition.

Aargh is a lengthening of "ah" to represent a prolonged cry.

An **abattoir** is a slaughterhouse for cattle.

A lazy monk is also called an **abbey-lubber**.

Abdabs or **habdabs** is a state of extreme nervousness or the jitters.

Abdomen is straight from Latin and originally denoted the fat deposited around the belly.

Aberuncator; to aberuncate is to pull up by the roots or extirpate.

To **ablaqueate** is to expose the roots of a tree by loosening or removing soil.

Ablatitious means "diminishing, lessening" a vowel change in related words – e.g. sing, sang, sung – is called an **ablaut** (from German *ab*, "off", and *Laut*, "sound") or **gradation**.

To **ablocate** means to rent or rent out.

Abnegate means renounce or reject something desired or valuable.

Abnormal means "not normal, different from normal" while **subnormal** means "below normal".

To **abraid** is to awake, arouse, or startle.

An **abreuvoir** is a space between bricks or masonry.

To **abvolate** is to fly away.

Acalculia is the inability to perform simple arithmetic.

Acatery are things bought or a storeroom for provisions, respectively.

To **accerse** is to summon.

Accismus is the pretended refusal of something that is actually coveted.

An **acclivity** is an upward slope.

Acclumsid is numb, paralyzed. Clumsy.

Acedia is spiritual sluggishness, indifference, or apathy.

Acedolagnia is complete indifference to sex.

An **acephalist** is someone who does not acknowledge a superior.

Acheron is another name for infernal regions or a river in Hell.

The original notion contained in the word **acid is** "pointedness".

Acrasia is acting against your better judgement or a lack of self-control.

Acrohypothermy is cold feet.

An ingrown nail is an **acronyx**.

An **actioner** is an exciting action-and-adventure film.

The word **"actor"** is preferred now for both men and women; **actor** was originally an agent or administrator and in Latin it meant "doer".

Acturience is the desire for or impulse to act.

Acuity pertains principally to hearing, vision, understanding, and wit.

Acumen suggests that keenness relates to a person's mind, whereas **acuity** suggests that it is related to a person's performance; **acumen** is something that a person has, whereas **acuity** is something that a person displays.

Adagio is music played "at ease".

Adidas is a blend of the first syllables of Adolf (Adi) Dassler, inventor of these athletic shoes.

Adnexa are the parts adjoining a human organ.

Adoxography is good writing on a trivial subject.

Adret is a mountain slope which faces the sun; the opposite is **ubac**.

An **aedicule** is a small room or structure used as a shrine– or a niche for a statue.

Aerometry is the measurement of airflow through the nose and mouth during speech.

Affluential is a blend of affluent and influential.

An **agape** is a love feast.

Agathism is the belief that things tend to work out for the better.

Agathokakological means "made of good and evil".

An **agelast** is a person who never laughs.

Agennesis is another word for impotence.

Agminate means "grouped together in a cluster".

Agnail is actually the torn skin around a fingernail (from Old High German *ungnagel*).

Agnoiology is the branch of philosophy studying human ignorance.

Agomphosis/agomphiasis is looseness of teeth.

Agrostology is the study of grasses.

Agrypnia is a synonym for insomnia; a fit of shivering is **ague**.

Akrasia is weakness of will (Greek o, "without," and *krator*, "power") when someone acts against their better judgement through weakness of will.

An **alector** is a person who is unable to sleep (from Homer's *Odyssey*).

Algesia is sensitiveness to pain.

Alieniloquy is a word for rambling or evasive talk.

Alimentotherapy is the assignment of dietary therapy to treat a disease.

Allodoxaphobia is a fear of others' opinions.

An **allograph** is a signature or writing done for another person.

If your feet are growing faster than your body as a whole, they are **allometric**.

Allopathy is treatment to suppress the symptoms of illness using the principle of opposites while **homeopathy** encourages rather than suppresses the body's reaction to an illness.

Allusion is an "indirect mention," **illusion** is "false impression," and **delusion** is "deception" which is much stronger than **illusion**.

Alogy is unreasonableness or absurdity.

Aloha is Hawaiian for both hello and goodbye and also means "love".

Alpenglow is the rosy lighting or the setting or rising sun as seen on high mountains.

Altoids (the breath mint) is from Latin *altus*, "highest, best," and *–oid*, an older pharmaceutical suffix.

Amalgamate seems to go back to Greek *malagma* "softening".

Amazon.com was so named because its founder wanted the store's inventory to be as deep and wide as the Amazon River.

Ambassador is based on Latin *ambactus*, "servant".

An **ambodexter** is an unethical lawyer or bribed juror.

Amentia is being out of one's mind with joy, in a rapturous daze.

Amiture is another word for friendship.

Amok is from a Malay *amuk*, "fighting furiously" or "rushing in a frenzy".

Among applies to things that can be separated and counted; **amid** cannot to things that.

Amphoric or **amphorous** is hollow-sounding, "like the sound made by blowing across the top of an open bottle".

Anaconda comes from a Sinhalese term for "whip snake".

An **analysand** is a person undergoing psychoanalysis.

Analysis is from Greek elements meaning "loosen up".

Anarchy is from Greek *anarkhos*, "without a chief".

Anaudia is loss of voice.

Anguria is a gourd or watermelon.

If one is **anhelous,** one is short of breath or panting.

Ankylosis is stiffness or immobility in a joint.

One's **anlage** is an inherited disposition to certain traits or a particular character development; **atavism** is the reappearance of characteristic after skipping one or more generations.

An **answer-jobber** is one who makes a living of writing answers.

Anthem is ultimately an alteration of *antiphon* "scriptural verse said or sung as a response- and they started out a composition from the Book of Psalms, then evolved to national (patriotic) anthems".

Anthology is from Greek *anthos*, "flower", so it a "bouquet" of literary pieces.

Anthropomorphism is the ascription of a human attribute or personality to anything impersonal or irrational.

Antibiotic is from *anti*, "against, not," and *biotikos*, "fit for life".

Antipastic means pertaining to appetizers or hors d'oeuvres (or the eating of them).

A word used in a sense opposite of the usual is an **antiphrasis.**

Anxiolytic means serving to reduce anxiety and **phrontifugic** is helping one escape one's thoughts or cares.

Anyway is correct if you mean "in any case", otherwise, use **any way.**

Apositic is "taking away the appetite".

Appetence is desire or longing.

Appetible is a synonym for desirable.

April is from Latin *operire*, "to open," *(aperia,* "open") as it is when trees unfold and the earth opens with new life.

Aprosexia is the inability to concentrate.

Aquose is a synonym for watery.

An **arborescence** is a treelike growth or formation.

Ardent means "burning, fiery" or "glowing like fire".

Armsaye or **armscye** (or **armseye** or **scye**) is the armhole in clothing, the hole in a shirt, sweater, jumper etc. through which you put your hand and arm.

Asbestos is from Greek words meaning "unquenchable".

Ascesis is the practice of self-discipline.

An **aspirant** is one who is seeking a higher position or some distinction.

Aspire comes from Latin *spirare*, "breathe" first meant "breathe into" or "rise, rise up".

Aspirin comes from, German *acetylierte Spirsaure* (acetylated salicylic acid).

Asterisk comes from the Greek word *aster*, "star," and it can be used to describe a little star or something starlike; **asterisk** should be pronounced AS-tuh-risk.

Astrometry is the precise measurement of celestial objects.

ATM machine is actually redundant, as the M stands for "machine".

Auctorial means "of or pertaining to an author".

Doctors look inside your ears with an **auriscope**.

Aurum is the Latin name for gold, from which its chemical symbol Au is derived.

Austral means "southern" while **boreal** means "northern" (as does **septentrional**).

Australia means "southern land".

Autograph comes from Greek words meaning "self" and "written".

Avatar can mean "manifestation" or "incarnation".

Avigation is a synonym for aerial navigation.

Avuncular means "behaving like or acting as an uncle."

Though **AWOL** stands for "absent without leave", no one is certain what the "o" stands for possibly the complete phrase was "absent without official leave".

Ayurveda is Sanskrit for "life science".

> The form of the letter **B** can be traced through early Greek to Phoenician and Egyptian hieratic

Babble is based on the repeated ba-ba-ba made by a **baby** or young child; **babe** and **baby** are also probably imitative of an infant's speech.

A backfriend is a secret enemy, a pretended or false friend.

Backwater is water fed by the backflow of a stream or river.

Baksheesh is a small sum of money given as a tip or as alms.

Balkan is derived from a Turkish word signifying "mountain".

Ballet is borrowed from French "little dance," the diminutive of *bal*, "dance".

Bamboo is ultimately derived from *Malay mamby*.

Banana comes from Arabic *banayna*, meaning "finger, toes," and bananas were once called Indian figs; the **banana** "tree" is really a giant herb with a rhizome instead of roots and its "trunk" is made of leaves, not wood.

Bandanna comes from Hindi *badhnu*, "tie-dyeing, cloth so dyed"; **bandanna** is the proper spelling, though bandana is acceptable.

Barbate means "bearded" and **barbatulous** is having a small beard.

Barber comes from Latin *barba*, "beard," because a **barber's** work consisted of trimming beards and originally they also performed surgery and dentistry.

Barbie's original name was Barbara, after the inventor's daughter.

Bated breath is based on the idea that the breath is abated or stopped.

Batik is Javanese, literally "painted".

Batter is based on a French word *bateure*, "action of beating".

BC means Before Christ, the years before the modern era of history, but now many use **BCE,** meaning Before Common Era; **AD** is *Latin* for Anno Domini, "in the year of our lord" to denote time after the birth of Christ, but many now use **CE** for Common Era.

Because is from the earlier "by cause," in turn based on French *par cause de*, by reason of, " and it originally meant "arrive, come".

A warning shock for an earthquake is a **before-shock**.

Bellboy first referred to a ship's boy who rang a bell.

Belly has its origin in *belig*, "skin bag", which was used to carry beans and peas.

Beret is based on Latin *birrus*, "hooded cape".

Beriberi is a Sinhalese reduplication of *beri*, "weakness".

Betroth is from the elements "be" and "truth", as in "be true to (somebody)".

Betweenity is another word for indecision.

Bibliobibuli are people who read too much.

A **biblioklept** is a book thief.

Bigamy breaks down to *bi-*, "*twice*" and *gamos*, "married".

Billet-doux, a love letter, is French for "sweet note".

Biscuit is Latin for *biscotum panem*, "twice cooked bread".

Bisque is an extra turn, point, or stroke allowed to a weaker player in croquet, court tennis, or golf.

A **blazer** was originally a brightly coloured ("blazing") jacket used in boating, cricket, and other sports.

Blog, formed by contraction of Web log (or weblog), is essentially an online personal diary or journal available to the public on a website.

Blunt originally meant "dull, obtus, foolish".

American humourist Gelett Burgess coined **blurb** – and he made a comic book with a character named Miss Blinda Blurb.

Bodacious is a blend of bold and audacious.

A **bodyscape** is a map of the body.

A joke that gets a hearty laugh is a **boffola**.

Bogus originally denoted a machine for making counterfeit money.

Bole is another name for the trunk of a tree.

Bombus is a buzzing in the ears, stomach, etc.

Bonbon is a French word for sweet.

Boodles is a great quantity, especially of money.

Bosh, "nonsense, foolish talk," is from Turkish *bos*, "empty, worthless".

Boss derives from the Dutch word *baas*, "master".

Both is from an Indo-European base meaning "each of two".

A **bottle** of wine is a **bottle** full of wine and a wine **bottle** is an empty **bottle** used to hold wine.

Bouquet comes from French *bosquet*, originally meaning "a little forest" or "clump of trees".

Bowel derives from Latin *botelluss*, diminutive of *botulus*, "sausage".

Branular means pertaining to or affecting the brain.

The meat of a boar is called **brawn**.

Brazen means belonging to or made of brass.

Breakfast literally means "breaking the fast" of the night, as it is the first meal after sleeping.

Bribe, from Old French, was originally a piece of bread given to beggars; the original sense of **bribe** is "extort, rob".

Brilliant can be traced to Italian *brillare*, "shine, shining".

When your glass or cup is filled to the brim, you have a **brimmer**.

Brown is a former name for a penny or any copper coin.

Brownette is a person who has light brown hair.

A **brunch** is the perfect name for a meal between breakfast and lunch.

Brunette is a diminutive of French *brun*, "brown".

Bucolic means "pertaining to country life; rural rustic".

Budget is derived from Old French *bougette*, "leather bag".

A **bugaboo** is something which one finds terrifying.

Bulldog is the first newspaper edition of the day, usually available the night before.

Bungalow, from Hindi *bangla*, "of Bengal, belonging to Bengal," was originally the house of a European in India—usually one storey with a veranda all the way around.

Burglar is literally a "town thief," ultimately from Latin *borgus/burgus*, "(walled) city," then Anglo-Latin *burgulator/ burglator*, and related to Old French *burgier*, "pillage".

Busboy is a person who clears the dirty dishes from diners' tables, so called from his "bus" or trolley.

Butler comes from French *boutellier*, "bottle or cup bearer" as originally it was an officer of high rank in charge of wine for the royal table (also Old French *bouteillier*, "a man who puts wine into bottles").

Butter derives from Greek *bouturon*, "cow," and *turos*, "cheese".

A **butty** is a slice of bread and butter.

Bylaw comes from *byr law*, "law or custom of a town" (*byr* = town) in Old Norse.

Nicknames were once **by names**.

Byte is a word formed arbitrarily from bit and bite.

A **byword** is a prime example.

> The form of the letter **C** is a rounding of the Greek *gamma*, which was the modification of the Phoenician sign for *gimel* "camel"

Cab is a shortening of cabriolet, which took its name from French *cabriole*, "goat's leap" —from the motion of the carriage.

The word **cabinet** originally meant a small room, and it came to apply to the group of politicians who met in the room.

To **cabobble** is to mystify, puzzle, or confuse.

Caboose originally signified the kitchen on merchant ships or fishing boats, having come from Dutch *kabuis*, "ship's gallery".

Cache first meant "a hiding place".

Cachexia is a chronically bad outlook or way of thinking.

Cacography is bad handwriting or poor spelling.

Cacology is a bad choice of words or poor pronunciation.

A **caconym** is a "bad name" or "bad terminology".

Cacophemism is the opposite of **euphemism**.

Caducity means "senility," "frailty," or "transitory nature".

Café is French for both coffee and coffee-house.

Cafeteria is literally Latin American Spanish for "coffee shop, coffeehouse".

Caffeine literally means "something found in coffee".

Cakewalk started out as a competitive dance and the winner of the **cakewalk** got a cake as a prize.

A person who draws with crayons is a **calcographer**.

Calculate comes from *calculus*, "a pebble used for counting and calculating".

Calid is another way of saying "warm, tepid".

Calisthenics comes from Greek *cali-*, "beauty, especially elegant" and *sthenos* "strong".

Calligraphy is from Greek meaning "beautiful writing".

Callus is a hard patch of skin; **callous** is an adjective meaning "indifferent to suffering" or "hardened".

Camcorder is a blend of video camera and video recorder.

Camisole derives from a diminutive of Latin *camisia*, "shirt or nightgown".

Camouflage derives from French *camou-flet*, "a puff of smoke".

Campus is "field" in Latin.

Can applies to what is possible and **may** to what is permissible; **can** means "able to," **may** means "permitted to".

Canapé is French for "couch, mosquito-netted sofa" or "covering" and is bread upon which other items sit for their being served before dinner.

Candid comes from Latin *candidus*, "white" and first meant "pure, innocent"; **candidate** is based on the same Latin word, and became Latin *candidatus*, "white-robed" as the traditional attire of a **candidate** for office was a white toga because it symbolised honesty.

Candle is from Latin *candere*, "to be white or glisten, to shine".

Candy comes into English from Arabic *qandi*, "sugar," which may be related to Sanskrit *khandokah*, "sugar in crystalline pieces" or *khanda*, "broken piece" applied to sugar pieces broken off a large block of crystallized sugar.

Canister comes from a word related to cane and originally was a basket for bread, fruit, or flowers.

A small can is a **cannikin;** a small pan is a **pannikin**.

Clinic first meant "teaching of medicine at the bedside".

Clinker is a stone-like furnace or coal residue.

Clinomania is an excessive desire to stay in bed.

Clo is the unit of measurement for the thermal insulation value of clothing.

Close, from Latin *clausum*, "closed place, first meant enclosure".

Closet first denoted a private or small room.

Cloud from Old English *clud* meant hill or rock at first, the name of a cloud describes both its appearance and its height above the ground.

A **cloudburst** is a torrential local downpour of rain of short duration.

Clout once meant "heavy blow".

Clown may derive from Northern Frisian meaning "clumsy fellow" or clod and it first referred to an unrefined person.

A **clutch** is a group of eggs laid in a single session.

Coal originally meant a glowing piece of wood or a cinder.

The difference between a **coast** and the **shore** is the **coast** is the seaward limit of the land and the **shore** is the landward limit of the sea.

The original senses of **coax** were fondle, pet or make a simpleton of.

Cobra is from Portuguese **cobra** de *capello*, "snake with hood" based on Latin *colubra*, "snake".

Coca-Cola is from *Quecha kuka*, "coca leaves, coca bush," borrowed via Spanish coca + cola from languages of West Africa *kola*, "cola nut".

Cockcrow is a literary word for dawn.

To **cockerate** is to brag.

A candy heart with a message is called a **cockle**.

In **cocksure**, cock is an euphemism for "God".

Cocktail is a drink sense for "adulterated" spirit.

If your Adam's apple is larger than normal, you are **cock-throppled**.

Cocoa is an alteration of Spanish *cacao*.

Coconut is the nut or seed of the coco-palm, from Portuguese *coco*, literally, "bogeyman," from the resemblance of a **coconut** to a grotesque head.

An egg cooked in water just below boiling is **coddled**.

A **codger** is a mildly eccentric person.

Codicil is a diminutive of *codex*, a "small part of a legal document," usually used to add to or change something about a larger piece of writing.

Coerce derives from Latin *arcere*, "restrain".

A **coffered** ceiling is one with ornamental sunken panels in a box like structure.

Coffin is French for "little basket"- from Greek *kophinos*, "basket," and first generally meant "box, case, casket, chest".

Cogitabund is being deep in thought.

Cognac is a name of a town in western France.

A blood relative is a **cognate**.

Cognomen is literally "name by which one is known".

Coin comes from the wedge-shaped tool or die (Latin *cuneus*, "wedge") that was used to hammer or stamp pieces of money.

Coincide can mean "occupy the same portion of space".

A word inventor is a **coiner** or **neologist**.

Coir is the fibre from the outer husk of a coconut.

A **col** is an area of low pressure between two high-pressure systems.

Cola is from Temne *k'ola*, "**cola** nut", cola seeds are used to make **Coca-Cola** and Pepsi-**Cola**.

When the moon is far to the north it is popularly called a **cold moon**.

Cold-blooded (*poikilothermic, poikilothermal*) is used for creatures whose blood takes on the temperature of their environment; **warm-blooded** (*homoiothrmic, homeothermal*) is having a fairly steady body temperature governed by the thermotaxic nerve mechanism.

Cold-fire is fuel laid for a fire, but unlit.

Beetle specialists are **coleopterists**.

Colic is, literally, "pertaining to the colon".

Collapse is a back-formation of collapsed.

Collar descends from Latin *collum*, "neck".

Collate first meant "to bring together for comparison; compare copies carefully" before it meant "put together sheets to make two or more copies of a document".

A **colleague** is literally "one chosen or delegated to be or work with another" and comes via French from Latin *collega* (*com-* "with" and *leg-* "choose").

The word **college** comes from Latin *collegium*, Legium, association, partnership, from college, partner in office. The word **university** is from Latin *universitas*, "the whole" from universus, "combined into one". The difference between a **college** and a **university** is that a **college** offers degrees in one or a few specific areas, while a **university** is a collection of colleges.

Collegial is the adjective for colleague.

Colletic means adhesive or adhesive substance.

Collocate is to place side by side.

Colloquial is Latin *col* and *loqui* speak and it describes a term used in ordinary or informal conversation.

Colloquy is a conversation (from Latin *colloquium*).

Collywobbles is a humorous term for stomach pain, queasiness, intense anxiety, or nervousness (from colic + wobble).

Cologne was created in **Cologne**, Germany and first called **Eau-de-Cologne** or **Cologne** water.

A **colon** (from Greek meaning "limb, member or clause of sentence") introduces a part of a sentence that exemplifies, elaborates, balances, or undermines the preceding part.

Colon the greater portion of the large intestine, comes from Greek *kolon*, "food meat".

Colonel comes from the Italian *colonna*, "column", from the arrangement of troops who were led by the head officer of a **regiment**; in Spanish it was *coronel* and it was so spelled in English at first and pronounced KORR-o-nel.

Colour refers to the wavelength composition of light; **shade** is a gradation of colour referring to its degree of darkness; **tint** is a gradation referring to its degree of lightness; and **hue** indicates a modification of a basic colour.

Baby seahorses are called **colts**.

Coma derives from Greek words translating to "lying down in bed."

Comb comes from *gombhos* (pre-Teutonic) for teeth, as the first combs were dried backbones or jawbones of fish.

A **comediographer** is a writer of comedies.

If something is tending to produce or aggravate acne, it is **comedogenic**.

Comedy comes from Greek *komos*, literally meaning "village bard or village merrymaker".

Comely is from a Dutch word *komlick*, fitting.

Come-on was first a slang term for a con man or swindler.

Comets, which have tails, get their name from Greek *kometes*, "long-haired star".

Comfort is from Latin *con*, an intensifier, and fortis, strong.

Comical is "funny unintentionally".

Comma (from Greek "a piece cut off") first meant a short clause or phrase within a sentence—and then came to be the name for the punctuation mark.

Commence is based on Latin *con-* (for emphasis) and *initiare*, "begin".

Commerce is another word for conversation.

Committee's original meaning was an individual to whom some charge, function, or trust is committed.

Commode is another word for toilet.

Commodity first meant "convenience, suitability" and then a "person's benefit, convenience, interest" and its Latin root meant "due measure, fitness, convenience, complaisance".

A **commonplace** book is a personal journal in which quotable passages, literary excerpts, and comments are written.

A **commorient** is a person killed in a disaster that claimed other lives.

Commuter came to mean any regular traveller to work.

Compact (adjective) can mean made up or composed of.

Companion is from French *compagnon*, "one who eats bread with another" from Latin *com*, with and *panis*, "bread".

A **companionway** is a stairway or ladder from a deck to the cabin below.

A **compare** is an equal or a rival.

A **compartment** describes a watertight division of a ship.

Compass (noun) first meant "cunning, cleverness, ingenuity".

Compathy is shared feeling.

Compendious means "abridged, succinct not voluminous".

Compete comes from Latin *competere*, "come together", but in later Latin it developed the sense strive together, which was the basis for the English term.

Competent once meant appropriate, suitable.

Competition refers to an abstract quality, whereas **competitiveness** implies a practical activity whose manifestation can be observed.

Compital means "pertaining to a crossroads".

Complacent means "pleased or satisfied with how things are, with "how they effect one's self"; **complaisant** means "attempting or eager to please or satisfy", "obliging, affable"—**Complacent** this refers to a state of mind and **Complaisant** to a disposition to behave or conduct oneself in a way that pleases or satisfies others.

Complain is from Latin meaning "to beat the breast" or "to lament".

Complement is "to complete, round out" and **compliment** is "to praise or admire" and as a noun it is an expression of praise or admiration.

Complicate, from Latin *plicare*, "fold", first meant "fold together, entangle, intertwine".

Component specifically implies that it is part of a machine or vehicle.

Deportment adds the sense of action or activity to a mode of conduct or behaviour; **Comportment** ("behaviour or bearing")

Compotation is another word for drinking session or drinking together.

A **compotator** is a drinking companion.

Compound meaning "combine comes from Latin *componere*, "put together"; **compound** the enclosure is from Malay *kam-pong*, "group of buildings; village" and come through Portuguese or Dutch.

Comprehend literally means "seize with the senses".

Comprise means literally "embrace". A zoo comprises of mammals, reptiles, and birds (because it "embraces" or includes them) but animals do not **comprise** (embrace) a zoo, they **constitute** a zoo.

Compromise started literally as a joint promise.

Comptroller is an erroneous speeling of controller; **comptroller** should be pronounced Kuhn-TROH-luhr.

A **compurgator** is a sworn witness to the innocence or good character of a person.

Compursion is wrinkling one's face.

Computeracy is a blend of computer literacy.

Computerate is another word for computer-literate.

Concentrate literally means bring toward or to a centre.

A **concern** is a complicated or cumbersome contrivance.

Conch comes from Greek *koghke*, "mussel; shell-like cavity", Latin *concha*, "shell" or "shellfish" and is either concha, and is either conchs or conches in plural; **conchology** is the study of shells and shellfish.

To **concinnate** is to put or arrange neatly; fit together skillfully.

Concise comes from Latin *concisus*, "brief" or "divided".

Conclave is based on *con-* and *clavis*, "key", as it was first an inner chamber or private room to which one would have needed a key, literally "a place that can be locked up" or a room or set of rooms that can be opened with only one key.

A **concomitant** is an accompanying thing.

Concord is literally "of one mind" in Latin.

A **concordance** is an index of all the words in a text, lined up by the keywords.

Condiment is from Latin *condimentum* from *condire*, to pickle, preserve; condiments are food substances used to heighten the natural flavour of foods, to stimulate the appetite, to aid digestion, or to preserve certain foods.

A **condisciple** is a fellow student.

Condole means to grieve over or grieve with.

Conduct first meant provision for a safe passage, such as an escort or pass, and the original form of the word was conduit.

Conductor was a term initially for a military leader.

Confectionery is sweets and chocolates collectively; **Confectionary** is a place where you buy confections.

A **conferee** is a recipient of an honour or a participant in a conference.

Conference first meant conversational talk.

Confess may apply to an admission of a weakness, failure, omission, or guilt.

Confetti is the plural of Italian *confetto*, "small sweet" as this was originally real or imitation bon-bons thrown during carnivals or after a wedding.

In **confide** and **confident**, part of the word is from Latin *fidere*, "trust".

Configure first meant "fashion according to a model".

Confirm first meant "make firm or firmer".

Confit is duck or other meal cooked slowly in its own fat.

One who confesses is a **confitent**.

Congeal (become semi-solid, especially upon cooling) is from Latin *con*, "together" and *gelare*, "freeze".

Congee is water in which rice has been boiled.

Congenial first meant kindered or sharing the same disposition.

Congenital means existing from birth while hereditary is "transmitted from one generation to another".

Congestion in the body is an accumulation of fluid.

Congratulate's etymology is *con-* and Latin *gratulari*, "manifest one's joy" and first meant to "celebrate with some act".

Conifer literally is Latin meaning "cone-bearing".

Another name for pink eye is **conjunctivitis**.

Conjure comes from Latin words meaning "band together by an oath, conspire"; it can also mean to beg or implore.

Conky is anybody with a big nose.

Connatural means "innate, belonging inherently or naturally to".

Little Red Book of Word Facts **25**

Connoisseur in French meant "knower, judge" and it indicates an expert in a particular area whose recognised knowledge and good taste have established his/her reputation.

Consensus came into English in a physiological "sense—a set of organs" or the "involuntary or reflex actions of the nervous system".

Connotation is from Latin *connotare*, "mark in addition".

Connubial is a synonym for "married, wedded".

Conscience is the noun meaning a "sense of right and wrong" while **conscious** is the adjective meaning "aware of something, being awake".

Consecrate's root is Latin *sacer*, "sacred".

Consecutive derives from Latin *consecut* "follow closely".

A **consequent** is a thing that follows something else in time or order, or following as a direct result.

Conservation is the creation of the environment in which a work of art is properly preserved.

Conserve once meant observe a custom or rite.

Conserves are jams thick with citrus fruit and nuts, possibly coconut or raisins.

Consider's root is from Latin literally "to study with the influence of the stars; to cast a horoscope".

A **consilience** is a chance happening or coincidence.

Consonance first meant "correspondence of sound in words or syllables".

A **consort** is a husband or wife or a monarch.

Conspire first meant "combine in action or aim", from Latin literally "breathe together".

Constable derives from Latin comes *stabuli* "count or officer of the stable".

Consfellation was first an astrological term, referring to the influence of planets and stars on events and personality.

Constipation is based on Latin elements meaning "press or come together".

Constitute can mean "make laws" and a **Constitution** is a "how-to" document for a government or organisation.

Constrain can mean "compel to do", "bring about by compulsion".

Construct was generalised from "piling up together" as in stones to make a house, to meanings like "piling up words to make a sentence" or "a group of words forming a phrase".

Construe first meant to "analyse the construction of a sentence" and "to explain the arrangement and meaning of words in a sentence".

A **consuetude** is a social custom or convention.

A **consulate** is essentially a junior embassy.

Contaminate seems to come from the base *tag* "touch", which became Latin contagmen, contact, and then Latin *contagmen*.

Conte is another word for adventure story.

Contemporary can be predicated of persons, conditions, or events; **contemporaneous** is predicable only of occurrences or events.

Contempt is a more engaged, more involved feeling of disapproval than disdain.

Contemptible means deserving contempt, while **contemptuous** means bestowing contempt; the first sense of contemptuous was "despising law and order".

Content comes from the Latin plural *contenta*, "things contained".

Contentment first referred to payment of a claim which "satisfied" the obligation.

Contiguous implies having contact on all or most of one side.

Continent is "able to control the bowels and bladder" or "exercising self-restraint".

Contingent suggests the possibility of happening but stresses uncertainty and dependence on other future events for existence or occurrence.

A **contour** line on a map passes through points of equal elevation or depth.

Contradict is from Latin *contra dicere*, "speak against".

Contralto is the voice intermediate between soprano and tenor.

Contrast was first used as a term in fine art; on a TV or computer monitor, it is a control that increases or decreases the difference between the dark and light areas of the screen.

Contrite is "bruised, crushed" or "worn or broken by rubbing".

Contrive was once *controve*, from Latin *contropare*, "represent metaphorically".

Control first meant "to check or verify accounts" and referred to a duplicate or keeping a copy; a **control** is the standard comparison in a statistical analysis or scientific experiment.

Contubernal is a tentmate or a person you live with, as an intimate companion.

Contusion comes from Latin *come* (intensive) and *tundere*, "beat, hit".

Conundrum first meant "whim" and then "pun" and then its current sense of "puzzling problem", the plural is **conundra**.

Convenience originally meant "suitability" or "commodiousness".

Convent originally applied to a body of monks, friars, or nuns that lived together.

Conventional usually expresses the unfavorable senses of "artificial" or "formal" or "old fashioned".

Conversation once had meanings "intimacy, familiarity" and living or way of life as it came from Latin *conversari*, "keep company with".

Converse is a noun meaning "social communication".

Convex (from Latin *convexus*, "arched vaulted") refers to a surface that curves outward concave (from Latin *concavus*, "hollow") to a surface that curves inward.

Convince started out meaning "overcome, conquer".

Cook came from popular Latin *cocus* from Latin *coquus*; to *cook* can mean to falsify concoct, make up.

Cookie comes from Dutch koekje, a diminutive of *koek* "cake".

Coop is based on Latin *cupa*, "barrel" and originally referred to a basket placed over fowl when sitting or being fattened (as in hen *coop*), hence the occupation of a cooper.

Coordinate first meant "of the same rank" or "place in the same rank".

Coot is a word for a silly person or simpleton.

Copious comes from Latin *copia*, "plenty" (as in cornucopia).

A **corbel** is a projection of stone, brick, timber, iron, etc., jutting out from the face of a wall to support something.

The notion behind **coppice** (dense growth of bushes) is of "cutting" and it comes from Greek *kolaphas*, "blow", which became Latin *colpare*, "cut".

Copra is the dried meat of the coconut.

A **copula** is a connecting word, especially forms of "be" linking a subject and complement.

Copy is based on Latin *copia*, "abundance, plenty".

Copyleft is an arrangement for artistic works or software in which they may be used and distributed on the condition that anything derived is bound by the same condition.

Copyright is, literally, "the right to reproduce" one's own work or authorise others to do so; *copyright* protects original artistic, literary, dramatic, musical, and intellectual work in a tangible medium.

Cordate means heart-shaped.

Cordial (literally "from the heart") translates (Latin *cordialis* from *cor(d)*, "heart") to drinks that are comforting or "invigorating the heart"; a synonym of **cordial** is liqueur.

A **correspondent** is a person charged with adultery.

A **corona** can be a small circle of light around the sun or moon.

Coronary comes from Latin *corona* "garland, crown" and it was applied to anatomical structures like arteries that encircle others like a crown–with the main example being the heart with its encircling blood vessels.

A **coroner** was once an official responsible for safeguarding the private property of the Crown (literally "guardian of the pleas of the Crown").

Corporation derives from Latin *corporare*, "combine in one body", or *corporatus*, formed into a body one's **corporation** is one's entire body of work.

Corpse originally meant a body or person, not one that was dead.

Corral is from Latin *currale*, "enclosure for carts".

Correct comes from Latin *corrigere*, "make straight; amend".

Correctitude is correctness of behaviour with adherence to rules of etiquette.

A **corrida** is a bullfight.

Corridor comes from an Italian word meaning "running place" as it runs from one place to another.

Corroborate was first recorded in the sense "make physically stronger".

Corrupt comes from Latin *corrumpere*, "destroy completely" and first meant "to destroy or spoil the flesh, fruit, or organic matter by dissolution or decomposition".

Cortex is a Latin word meaning bark to **coruscate** is to give forth intermittent or vibratory flashes of light, to shine with a quivering light–as light does between the trees as one drives along a road.

A cluster of ivy berries or grapes is a **corymb**.

Coryza is a head cold.

Co-sleeping is when parents allow a child to sleep in their bed.

Cosmetics comes from Greek *kosmetikos*, "skilled in decorating from *kosmein*, "arrange, adorn".

Cosmolatry or **physitism** is the worship of nature.

Cosmos is from Greek *kosmos*, "order of world" and is often used to suggest an orderly or harmonious universe.

A **costa** is a rib or riblike structure.

Cost-benefit refers to assessing the benefits of an undertaking in relation to its cost.

Cost-effective is anything effective and productive in relation to its cost.

Costermonger is, literally, apple dealer.

Costume and **custom** were actually two forms of the same Latin root *consuetudinem*, habit, **custom**, with **costume** first meaning "manners and customs belonging to a particular time and place".

Something that **costs** a particular amount literally "stands at or with" that price (Latin *constare*, "to be settled or fixed, stand at a price, **cost**").

Cot is ultimately derived from Sanskrit *khatva*, "bedstead, couch, hammock", then Hindi *khat*, and was first a small cottage or humble dwelling.

A **cote** is a shelter for birds or mammals.

A **coterie,** from French, is literally "tenants holding land together" and now a circle of persons who associate with one another, as distinguished from "outsiders"; a **coterie** is also a group of prairie dogs occupying a communal burrow.

Cotton is actually from Arabic *qutun*.

Cough is of onomatopoeic origin.

Coulrophobia is the fear of clowns.

Council comes from Latin words meaning "summon" and "together".

Counsel is "advice, guidance" and a **Counsel** is a lawyer; a **council** is a deliberative body of people assembled for some purpose and members are **councillors**.

Countenance is the face together with its expression–and the mood or character which is revealed; to **countenance** is to sanction or support.

The **counter** on a shoe is the stiff piece of leather backing the heel.

Counterfeit once meant a legitimate copy.

Counterpane is a coverlet for a bed, such as a quilt or bedspread.

Country really refers to geographical characteristics while **nation** refers to political and social characteristics; **country** comes from Latin *contrata (terra,)* "the landscape in front of one" the landscape lying opposite to the view and **nation** is from Latin nation/nation race, class of person".

County acquired via Anglo-Norman counte from French *counte* "land belonging to a count", first meant a meeting held periodically to transact the business of a shire.

Coup was first a blow or stroke, from Greek *kolaphos*, "blow with the fist".

A **coupe** is defined as a closed, two-door, two-seat motor car and is short for French *carosse coupe* "shortened coach".

Coupon is French for "piece cut off" and originally denoted detachable portion of a bond to be given in return for payment of interest; **coupon** should be pronounced KOO-pon.

Courage comes from Latin *cor*, "heart" and denotes this as the seat of feelings.

Courbette is when a trained horse rears up and jumps forward on the hind legs.

Courier is based on Latin *currere*, "to run". Etymologically, *course* denotes "running" from Latin *currere*, run, and the earliest meaning was "onward movement in a particular direction".

Court comes from Latin *cohors*, "enclosed yard".

Courteous first meant "having manners fit for a royal court".

A **coven** is a gathering of witches, especially thirteen of them.

Cover ultimately comes from Latin *cooperire*, *com-* "completely" and *operire* "**cover**".

Covert (concealed, covered, hidden) is the opposite of **overt** (apparent, open to view, plain, public).

Coward is literally French *cove*, "tail" (from Latin *cauda*, "tail"), + *ard*, "tail person", because a frightened animal "turns tail" or has its tail between its legs.

Cowl is the section of a car that holds the windshield and dashboard.

The **coxcomb** is the cap worn by a professional fool.

A **coxswain** was originally a servant (swain) whose job it was to steer a boat (cock or cockboat).

To **cozen** is to cheat, dupe, beguile, defraud besides a tea **cozy**, there are egg **cozies**.

Crab comes from Old English *crabba* and Old Norse *krabbi*, "to scratch and claw".

Crack the drug, got its name because it crackles when you smoke it.

The "**crack**" of a whip is a miniature sonic boom as the tip breaks the sound barrier.

Crackpot was originally "cracked pot".

Crapula is a synonym for hangover and **crapulent** or **crapulous** mean drunk words for feeling ill from overeating or drinking are **crapulent**, **crapulous**, **cropsick**.

Crastin is the morrow or the day after.

To **crastine** is to put off from day to day.

Crater comes from Greek *krater*, "mixing bowl".

Crayon derives from French *craie*, and earlier Latin *creta*, "chalk clay"; in art, a **crayon** is any drawing material in stick form.

Crazy goes back to a Scandinavian word *krasa*, "broken".

Creative was coined in association with art, not with the divine.

Crebrous means frequent.

Creed comes from Latin *credo*, "I believe".

Creek has the root sense "crooked water-way" (from Old Norse *kriki*, "crook, twist").

Corpuscular is "of or like twilight".

Crestfallen is an allusion to fighting cocks whose crests fall in defeat and rise in victory.

Cricket's (the game) name is derived from French *criquet*, "goal post, wicket".

A vehicle or ship unfit for service is a **cripple**.

Criterion comes from Greek *criterion*, "means of judging".

Critic and **crisis** both ultimately come from Greek *kritos*, "judge, discern" and then *kritikos*, "able to make judgments and one who makes judgments, which passed into Latin *criticus* and then to English **critic**.

Crochet is from French little hook (diminutive of *croc*, "hook") which is what is used for such needlework.

Crockery gets its name from the obsolete *crocker* "potter".

Crocodile is based on Greek *krokodilos*, "worm of the stones".

Crocodility is false reasoning.

A **crone** is a very old woman.

Crowbar gets its name from the two-pronged end that resembles the foot of a crow.

Crucify comes from Latin *cruai figere* "fix to a cross" and **crucifix** comes from Latin *crucifixus*, "fixed to a cross".

Cruise probably comes from Dutch *kruisen*, "to cross".

Crumbs is an expression of astonishment or dismay.

Crux originated as a reference to a real cross and its association with torment and trouble.

Cry comes via old French *crier* from Latin *quiritare*, "call for the help of the Quirites" (those who held the rank of Roman citizen).

Crypt is from Greek *kryptos*, "concealed".

Cryptic comes from Greek *kryptikos*, "hidden".

A **cryptonym** is a code name or secret name.

Cuckold is a derivative of cuckoo, the cuckoo's invasion of other birds' nests perhaps being viewed as analogous to the stealing of a wife's affections by another man.

The **cuckquean** is the female counterpart of the cuckold.

Cuisine is French for "kitchen" and first meant that or "a culinary establishment".

Culinary should be pronounced KYOO luh-ner-ee but many say KULL-uh-ner-ee (from Latin *culinarius*, "kitchen").

Cultured refers to people and pearls.

Cultivated refers to mind, tastes, speech, or behaviour.

Curfew comes from French *coevefru/cuevre-fu* "cover the fire" from the medieval regulation of the time by which fires had to be extinguished in the evening, which was indicated by the ringing of a bell.

Curl is disease of plants in which the leaves or shoots are curled up and not developed perfectly.

Curriculum, from Latin *currer* "to run" evolved into "to run a course" and then to the full slate of courses offered for study.

Curry is from Tamil *kari*, "sauce"–as it first meant spicy sauce for wheat cakes or rice.

Cursive comes from Latin *currere*, "to run" and it means running hand, writing in which the pen is not raised after each character.

Cursor first meant "runner" or "running messenger" and now it is the moving/movable indicator on a computer screen.

Cursory means "superficial" **cursorial** is "pertaining or adopted to running".

Curt is from Latin *curtus* "abridged, cut short".

Cutlery includes knives but there is no association with cut, rather being from old French *coutelier*, cutler's art from *countel*, knife.

Cybernetics was coined in French as *cybernetique* in the 1830s but meant "art of governing", and in English it came to mean "theory of control and communication processes."

Cyclone probably comes from Greek words meaning "circle eye"; it is the general term for a storm that can be called, depending on features and where it occurs, a hurricane, typhoon, or tornado.

Not quite a manic-depressive but with tendencies in that direction is a **cyclothyme**.

Cygnet is literally a "small swan from Latin *Cygnus*, "swan" The adjective form of swan is **cygnine**.

Cylinder derives from Greek *kulindein*, "to roll".

A **cynologist** is a dog trainer.

Cynophobia is the morbid fear of dogs.

A **cynosure** is an admired person or thing, the focus of attention; the base of **cynosure** is "dog's tail"—referring to the star called *Polaris* (North Star), a reference point for mariners.

The letter **D** is from the shape of a doorway or archway

Daft first meant crazy and silly.

A horse's mother is a **dame**; dam; the father is a **sire**.

Damage comes from Latin *damnum* "**damage** loss".

Damp (the noun) first meant vapour, steam or "smoke"—especially that was harmful or noxious.

Daredevil is a contraction of "someone ready to dare the devil".

Darling derives from "dear".

Daze is from Old Norse and first meant "exhausted from cold or exertion".

D-Day actually means "day day" as redundancy was common in military correspondence referring to a top-secret time.

Deadline is a Civil War term for a line that marked the distance a prisoner could go before being shot on sight.

A **deadlock** was first a lock with no spring catch.

In **deadpan,** pan means "face".

Deal first meant a part, portion, or division of a whole.

Dean comes from Latin decanum, "chief of a group of ten", and Greek *dekanos*, "a monk or dignitary in charge of ten others".

Dearth means "scarcity", not complete lack.

To **deasil** is to travel in the direction of the sun.

Death means "act or process of dying".

Debate is from Latin *de*, down, completely" and *battere*, "to fight, beat".

Debenture is from Latin *debenture*, "there are due".

Debility comes from Latin *debilis*, "weak", and has no connection with the word ability.

Debonair comes from Old French "*de bonne aire*" meaning "of good disposition".

Debris comes from French *de-* and *briser*, "break".

Debt is based on Latin *debere*, "owe".

A **debut** is a first public appearance; a **premiere** is a first performance, showing, or broadcast.

Decease actually means "departure from life", from Latin *decessus*, "departure".

December was originally so named because it was the tenth month in the Roman calendar, derived from Latin *decem*, "ten".

Decibel is literally one-tenth of a bel, a unit of sound intensity.

Deciduous derives from Latin *deciduus*, "falling down".

Decimal is from Latin *decimus*, tenth from *decem*, "ten".

Decimate means "to destroy in part", not entirely; the literal and original sense of *decimate* was put to death one person in ten".

Decipher can also be spelled *decypher* and it first meant "discover, find out;" a synonym is *decrypt*.

Declivity is a fancy name for a downward slope.

Decorate suggests relieving plainness or monotony by adding beauty through colour or *design*.

Decrease literally means "ungrow" (Latin *decrescere*).

Decry is literally to "cry down", i.e. "denounce, condemn".

Decumbiture is the act of going to bed when sick.

Deduce first meant "to lead" (from Latin *ducere*, "to lead").

Defatigable is apt to or capable of being wearied.

Defenestration is the act of throwing someone out the window (French *fenestra*, "window").

Defer is from Latin *differre*, "to carry apart, delay".

Defervescence is cooling down.

Defile is an alteration of defoul, "to trample down, to tread on".

Define comes from *de-* "completely, thoroughly" and *finire*, "finish", and firt meant bring to an end, settle–hence, **definite**.

Defuse means to remove a fux–usually from an explosure.

Defy first meant renounce faith.

Deglutition is the act of swallowing.

Degressive mens "reducing by gradual amounts".

Deity comes from Latin *dues*, "god"

To take an oath is to **dejerate**.

A late breakfast can be called a **dejeuner deke** is a shortened form of decoy.

Deleterious is based on a Greek word for "noxious".

Deletitious means pertaining to erasing.

Delibation is a taste or sip.

Delicious is the underlying meaning of "tempting luring from the straight and narrow", from Latin *delicia*, "delight".

Delight is from French *delitier* from Latin *delectare*, "to charm" and the change in spelling to "*gh*" was patterned on words like "light".

Deliver comes from latin *de-* "away" and *liberare*, "liberate, set free".

A **dell** is a small, secluded valley.

Deltiology is collecting or studying postcards.

Deluxe, once two words, is French for "luxury".

Demeanor comes from the obsolete verb *demean*, "behave".

The **denominator** in a fraction is the part below the horizontal line (called the **separatrix**) and the **numerator** is above the line.

Demolish comes from Latin *de-* and *moliri*, "construct".

The reading of tree rings for dating purposes is **dendrochronology**.

Dentiscalp is a fancy word for toothpick.

Depend first meant "hang down, be suspended from", as an icicle.

Depict first meant "represent in colours".

Depot can mean "act of depositing".

Derelict comes from Latin *de* "completely" and *relinquere* "leave, forsake".

The **dermis** is also called the true skin and it forms the bulk of the thickness of the skin.

Desert is from Latin *desertum*, "something left to waste" and implies that the object left may be weakened but not destroyed by one's absence.

Deserve is from Latin *deservire*, "serve well or enthusiastically".

Design was first a plan or scheme.

Desire literally began as "to examine the stars carefully–based" on Roman beliefs in astrology.

Dessert comes from a French word that means "clear the table" as it is the course served at the end of a meal.

Desserts are sweets; **deserts** is something deserved.

Etymologically, one's **destiny** is that which has been firmly established or determined for one, as if by fate.

Detect originally meant "uncover" and "expose".

Détente is an "easing of tensions" and **entente** means "understanding".

Determine is based on Latin *de*, completely and *terminare*, "set bounds to".

Detest originally meant "to bear witness against".

Detonate is from Latin *detonare* "thunder down, cause to explode".

Detumescence is the subsiding of swelling.

Deuterogamy is one's second marriage.

Devil is from Greek *diabolos*, "accuser, slanderer".

The **dewlap** is the loose fold of skin below the throat in cattle, dogs, etc.

Dharma means "something established; decree, custom" from Sanskrit.

A **diagnosis** is the process of idenfiying or determining the nature of a diseased condition or the conclusion reached; a **prognosis** is a prediction of the probable course of a disease or likely outcome of a problem.

Diameter is from Greek meaning "measure through" (a circle or sphere, etc.)

Diapason, a grand swelling harmony is literally "through all (notes)".

Diarrhoea is made of Greek elements *dia*, "through" and *rhein*, "to flow".

Diary can mean "lasting for one day" or "ephemeral".

To **dibble** means "to drink like a duck", lifting up the head after each sip.

Diction first meant simply "word" or "phrase".

Didactics is the art of science of teaching one who disappears and then pops up again is a **didapper**.

Diet comes from Greek *diaita*, "a way of life, mode of living".

Different is from Latin *differre*, "carry apart, separate".

Digamy is a second marriage, **trigamy** a third, and **quadrigamy** a fourth.

A **digestif** is an alcoholic drink taken to aid digestion.

Dignity can be a synonym for **dignitary**

A distinguishing mark or sign can be called a **dignotion**.

To **dilate** is to write or speak about at great length.

A **dimble** or **dingle** is a deep and shady dell or hollow.

Dimension derives from Latin *di-* and *metiri*, measure.

Diminish is a blend of *diminue*, "speak disparagingly" and *minish*, "reduce in amount, degree, influence, power".

Dimple first meant "hollow in the ground" before "hollow in the cheek".

Dine and **dinner** come from French *denser*, from *desjeuner*, "to break a fast"; in Middle English **dinner** meant "breakfast" or "fist big meal of the day".

Dinful means noisy.

A **dingo** is wild Australian dog.

Diocese is based on Greek words meaning "administer, keep house". (*oikos* "house")

Disaster is from Italian *disastro*, literally "ill starred event" and was first "the influence of an unlucky planet or evil star".

Diplomat is Greek for "folded twice" as a person dealing in secret matters needed to take this precaution with documents.

Dipsomania is an insatiable desire for alcoholic beverages.

Disappoint originally meant "remove from a post or office".

Disastrous is literally "ill-starred" (*dis* "bad" and *astrum*, "star").

Discard first meant "throw out or reject a card from a hand".

Disclose once meant "to open, to hatch".

Disco in Latin means "I learn".

A **discography** is a list of musical recordings by a person or group.

Discord is literally "severance of hearts", from Latin *Discordia* (cord "heart").

Discotheque is French originally meaning "record library".

Discreet means "judicious, prudent, showing discernment", while **discrete** means "detached, separate" and "individually distinct".

Disease originally meant "uneasiness; annoyance".

In **disgruntled**, *dis*- means "twice and *gruntle* is grunt complain) repeatedly hence double gruntled".

Disgust is, literally, "have no taste for", "have strong distaste for".

Dish is a more general term and **plate** is more specialised.

To **disheir** is to deprive of an heir, to stop a lineage.

Dishabille and **discinct** mean loosely dressed or partly undressed.

Dishevelled is based on *dis*, "not" and old French *cheval*, "hair" and the first meaning was "wearing nothing on the head".

Disinflation means the rate of inflation is going down and prices are rising but at a slower pace; **deflation** means that prices are going down–which is negative inflation.

Disinformation is that which is deliberately misleading.

If you are **disinterested** you have no stake in the outcome of an event and you are impartial–but if you are **uninterested** you simply don't care **disinterested** is "impartial, neutral" and **uninterested** is "bored, lacking interest".

Dispense is ultimately from Latin *dispendere*, "weigh out".

Display first meant "to unfold", coming from Latin *dis* and *plicare* "fold".

Disrupt first meant "break apart, separate forcibly".

To **dissect** language is to parse it–as analysing the structure of a sentence.

Dissemble means to conceal, to give a false appearance; **disassemble** means to take apart.

Dissertation is from Latin literally "continue to discuss"; to **dissert** is to discuss or examine.

Distort first meant "twist to one side".

Distrait means "absent-minded as a result of apprehension, worry, etc." while. **Distraught** means "agitated" and "bewildered, distracted".

To **distrust** is to suspect someone is dishonest; to **mistrust** is to merely lack confidence in someone.

Dictionary is based on Latin *dictio(n)*, "mode of expressions" or "word".

Ditto is from Italian *ditto*, "said aforesaid, spoken", and is abbreviated do, or expressed by two dots or commas or a dash.

A **dittology** is a double reading or interpretation.

Disturb is based on Latin *turba*, "tumult", and **disturb** applies better to physical agitation and **perturb** to mental agitation.

A **dividend** can be a portion or share of anything divided.

DNA is the prime constituent of chromosomes and it controls the hereditary characterstics and synthesis of proteins within the cells of virtually all living beings; **RNA** is a complex nucleic acid in cells, that is involved in the synthesis of protien.

To **doattee** is to nod the head when sleep comes on while one is sitting.

Doctor in Latin means "teacher".

Docity is the ability to learn quickly.

Document first meant "instruction" or "evidence", whether written or not.

Dogfall is a draw or tie.

Doggerel is loosely styled verse with an irregular rhythm, usually intended to be comical.

An orphaned calf is a **dogie**.

Dogma is Greek for "opinion", but now it means principle (s) laid down as incontrovertible.

Dolor is mental pain or suffering, but it first meant physical pain.

Something that relieves or drives away sadness is **dolorifuge**.

A **domestic** animal is a pet a **domesticated** animal is a formerly wild animal bred for human use.

Domino was once slang for the teeth and also for the keys of a piano.

Doppelganger is borrowed from a German word meaning "double-goer".

Do-si-do is an alteration of French *dos-a-dos*, "back-to-back".

Dossier comes from French denoting a bundle of papers in a wrapper with a label on the back (from *dos*, "back" based on Latin *dorsum*).

Dot first meant the "head of a boil" or "small lump or **dot**".

A person is capable of **doubting**, whereas a thing is **dubitable**; dubious, unlike **doubtful**, carries the connotation of suspicion.

Dote comes from a Dutch word meaning "to be silly".

Doubt is from Latin *dubitare*, "to go two ways of once" or "to move from one side to the other".

To be **doughty** is to be capable, fearless, valiant, and worthy.

Afternoon drinking is called **doundrins**.

A **dowager** is a wealthy widow.

Doxastic means "pertaining to an individual's beliefs".

A **doxology** is a shart utterance of praise to God, such as the "Gloria Patri".

Drama is literally "that which is done", from Greek **drama** "deed, action".

Originally **draper** was a dealer in cloth only, derived from French *drap*, "cloth".

Drapetomania is an intense desire to run away from home.

Dreamt is the only English word that ends in "mt".

Drier is the adjective; **dryer** is the appliance.

Drizzle is defined as 14 drops per square foot per second; light rain is 26 drops per square foot per second.

Droll means "unintentionally funny".

Drone derives from an Old English word for "male bee", from a Germanic verb meaning "resound; boom".

To **drowse** is to be half asleep or to doze the etymological notion of **drowsy** seems to be heaviness.

To **drumble** is to move in a slow, sluggish way.

A small chicken wing that resembles a **drumstick** is a **drumette**.

Dry-roasted means roasted without fat or oil.

DSL stands for digital subscriber line.

Duck comes from Old English duke, diver.

Dull originally meant "slow-witted".

A **duologue** is a lengthy conversation between two people.

A **duplet** is a set of two things.

DVD stands for digital versatile disk.

To **dwizzen** is to shrink and dry up or look parched.

Dynasty is from Greek *dunasteia*, "domination, power".

Dysentery derives from Greek *dus*, "bad" and *entera*, "bowels".

Dyslogistic is expressing disapproval.

Dyspathy is antipathy–either dislike or disagreement in feeling.

> Easily the most–often-used letter in English-language print, **E** outdistances runners-up T, A and I by a wide margin. One reason is the many shades (about 15) of vowel sounds E can represent

An abrupt tide rise is an **eagre**.

A mug's handle is the **ear**.

A small box of information at the top of a newspaper's front page is an **ear**.

Early is based on *ere*, "before".

Earnest was first a noun meaning "seriousness of feeling".

Earth the planet is capitalised, while.

Earthenware is low-fired clay.

Porcelain is high-fired, **stoneware** is about halfway between **earthenware** and **porcelain** in quality and durability, and the terms **china** can be applied to any **porcelain earthenware** or ceramic ware dishes or crockery.

Eatertainment is dining combined with entertainment.

Ebriety is another word for drunkenness.

Ebullition is a sudden outburst of emotion or violence.

Ecceity is "the quality of being present".

Éclair is French for lightning bolt–perhaps for the speed with which one is eaten.

Ecology fomes from Greek *okologie*, from *oikos*, "home, habital" and ology.

Economic means "pertaining to the production and use of income" and **economical** is "avoiding waste, being careful of resources".

Eczema is from Greek *ekzema*, "eruption".

Edacious means pertaining to eating; **Edacity** is a voracious appetite.

Edentate means "without teeth".

Edit first meant "give it out, put out, publish" **edit** as in "prepare for publication" is a back-formation from editor.

Editor is a Latin word meaning "producer (of games), publisher" from *edere*, "to put out, produce".

Effort first meant power and it comes from Latin *ef* and *fortis*, "strong".

Effrontery is from Latin *effrons*, "barefaced, shameless".

Effulgent means "shining brilliantly"

An **eft** is a small lizard or lizard-like animal, like a *newt*.

An **egeria** is a female advisor.

Eggplant was so named because the delicate white varieties resemble eggs.

Eisegesis is the interpretation of a word or passage by reading into it one's own ideas.

Either is the descendant of an ancient Germanic phrase meaning "always each of two".

Elbow-lifting is an euphemism for a fondness for drinking.

Eldorado means "the gilded one".

Election came via French from Latin *electionem* from the earlier *eligere*, "to choose, pick out".

Electron is actually a combination of electric and on.

Elevate from Latin *elevare*, "to raise", is based on levis, light.

Elicit comes from a Latin stem meaning "draw forth by magic or trickery".

Eligible means fit or entitled to be chosen and comes from Latin *eligere* "choose".

Elude comes from *e* "out, away from" and *ludere*, "to play".

Elusion is the action of deluding someone–or an escape or evasion.

Emacity is an urge to buy.

Embolalia are useless or hesitation words or utterances in speech like oh, uh, you know, I mean.

Embonpoint means plumpness, though in French *en bon point* means "in good shape".

Embrace's source is Latin *in* and *brachium*, "arm" and the word implies a ready or happy acceptance.

Embryo comes from *em*, "into" and *bruein*, "swell, grow".

Emerge is a combination of *e-* "from" and Latin *merge*, to dip, plunge".

Emesis is a kinder word for vomiting and an *emetic* is a substance causing vomiting.

The **Emmy** Award is an alteration of Immy, nickname for image orthicon, a camera tube used in television production.

Emote is derived (a back-formation) from emotion.

Empathy denotes a deep emotional understanding of another's feelings or problems, while **sympathy** is more general and can apply to small annoyances or setbacks.

Emporeutic is pertaining to merchandise or to trade.

Emporium is from a Greek word for "merchant".

Empressement is a show of affection.

Encomium means "high praise".

Encore is French for "again" or "still".

Encyclopedia comes from Greek *enkuklios*, "all-around, general" and *paideia*, "education".

To **endue** is to put on an item of clothing.

Endure first meant "harden, strengthen" and its Latin roots are *en-* and *durus*, "hard".

Engorge come from French *en-* "into" and *gorge*, "throat".

Enhance originally meant "elevate", both literally and figuratively.

An **enigma** was originally a riddle, usually involving metaphor, from Greek *ainigma*, "riddle" from *ainos*, "fable".

Enjoy probably comes from Old Frech *enjoir* "in rejoice".

An **enophile** or **oenophile** is a connoisseur or lover of wines.

To **ensanguine** is to stain with blood.

Ensemble means "at the same time, together" and is from *in* and Latin *simul*, "at the same time".

Ental means inner or inside.

The state of actuality is **entelechy**, as opposed to **potentiality**.

Enter's Latin base is *intra*, "within".

Enthasy is a soft, quiet death.

Enthuse is a back-formation of enthusiasm.

Enthusiasm, from Greek *enthous*, first meant "possessed or inspired by a god".

Entomology the science of bugs/insects-is based on Greek *entomos*, "insect".

A light dish served between two courses of a formal meal or dishes served in addition to the main course of a meal is **entremets**.

Epalpabrate means "without eyebrows".

Epeolatry is the worship of words.

Epics are long poems about legendary heroes; **sagas** are prose epics about famous men and women especially of medieval times.

Epilogue is taken from Greek epilogos from *epi* "in addition" and *logos*, "speech".

The **epimyth** is the moral of a story.

Epincian means "celebrating victory".

Epiphany was originally the appearance or manifestation of a divinity.

Episode, first a Greek dialogue between two songs, is from *eis*, "into" and *hodos*, "way".

Epistaxis is a word for nosebleed.

Epistemology is the theory or science of the methods or grounds of knowledge.

Epistle is from Greek *epistole*, "something sent to someone".

Epistolary means "of the nature of letters, contained in letters".

Epitaph is from Greek *epi*, "upon, over" and *taphos*, "tomb" or "funeral".

A poem written to celebrate a wedding is an **epithalamium**.

An **epopt** is an overseer, watcher, or beholder.

An **epulation** is a feast.

Equator comes from Latin *aequator*, "in full", *circulus aequator diet et noctis*, "circle equalizing day and night".

Equestrian comes from Latin *eques*, horseman from *equus*, "horse".

An **era** is a system of numbering years from an important event.

Erenow means "before this time".

An **ergophile** is a person who loves to work.

A two-year-old canary is an **eriff**.

Erotic comes from Eros, the winged god of love.

Erotology is the "science of love".

Erratic comes from Latin *errare*, "to stray, err".

To **ert** is to incite, urge on, encourage.

An **eructation** is a belch.

Erupt is literally "break out".

Esculent means "fit to be eaten".

Especially means "particularly" or "exceptionally" while **specially** means "for a specific purpose" **especially** comes from Latin meaning "belonging to a particular species", it now is restricted to mean "important".

Espionage is based on French *espion*, spy.

Espresso is strong black coffee; **cappuccino** is espresso to which foamy steamed milk has been added.

Essence is from Latin *esse*, "be".

The base of **establish** is Latin *stabilis*, "stable".

Esteem and **estimate** are from Latin *aestimare*, "assess, estimate".

Estrange is based on Latin *extraneus*, "not belonging to the family".

Etiology is the study of causes, origins, or reasons.

Etiquette is almost literally just the ticket.

Eudemonics or **eudemonism** is the art or a means of acquiring happiness or a theory of happiness.

Eugeria is a normal and happy old age.

An individual cane or shoot of bamboo is a **eulm**.

Euthanasia is from Greek *eu*, "well" and *thanatos* "death".

Evangelism is from Greek *euangelion*, "gospel or good news".

Event is from Latin *e* "out of" and "*venire*, "come".

Every is literally a compound word meaning "ever each".

Everyday is an adjective and it means "casual" or "informal" with an implied contrast to formality, as well as the meaning of "familiar, ordinary" in contrast with "strange, unusual"; the time expression is written separately **every day**.

Everyone is correct if you can substitute the word everybody–as it is a noun that means every person, "**every one** is a pronoun meaning "each one".

Evict first meant "conquer, overcome".

Evidence is information that helps form a conclusion; **proof** is factual information that verifies a conclusion.

To **evince** is to indicate, to reveal the presence of a quality or feeling.

If something is **evitable**, it is avoidable.

An **ewer** was a wide mouthed water jug formerly used in bedrooms.

Exact was first a verb, from Latin *ex*, "thoroughly" and *agere* "perform".

Exaggerate once meant "accumulate, pile up".

Exalt means to elevate, praise, or raise a person or thing; **exult** means to rejoice greatly.

An **exaltation** is a group of larks in flight.

An **examen** is a critical study.

Except is from Latin *ex*, "out of" and *capere*, "take".

Excerpt derives from Latin *ex-* "out of" and *carpere*, to pluck.

Exchange comes from Latin *cambire*, "barter".

Excruciating root sense is "to crucify".

Excuse is from Latin *ex-* out, out and *causa*, "cause blame, accusation".

An **exeat** is a leave of absence.

Execute derives from Latin *exsequi* "carry out, follow up punish".

Executive first meant "pertaining to execution putting something into effect".

An **exegesis** is an analysis of a word.

Exemplify can mean "make an official copy of a document".

Exfodiate means to dig out.

Exhume is from Latin *ex-* "out of" and *humus* "ground".

Exigency is anything needed, demanded, or required.

Expand comes from Latin *ex* "out" and *pandere* "to spread".

Expedient means "convenient in the circumstances" and suggests unfairness or dishonesty.

Expedite comes from a Latin word (literally "free the feet") meaning "put in order by freeing from difficulties".

Expedition retains the notions of speed and purpose.

Expenditure refers to an actual outlay of money or goods, whereas *expense* has a more general sense, a charge or cost of goods or property we have expenses, but we make expenditures.

Experience and **experiment** and **expert** derive from Latin *experiri*, "try".

Experrection is waking up or awakening.

To **expiate** is to make amends or reparation for.

Exponent as an adjective means "expounding, interpreting".

Extempore was literally "out of the time" in Latin.

A synonym for astonishing is **extonious**.

Extort and extortion are from Latin *ex* "out" and *torquere*, "to twist".

Extra is probably a shortening of extraordinary.

Extreme and **extremity** are from Latin *exter* "outer".

Exult is from Latin *ex* "out, upward" and *salire* "to leap".

> Forever related with obscenity, the letter F can seem vulgar or comical by itself. F's crude sound attracted comment even before English was born. Cicero called it the "unsweetest" sound in Latin.

A **fainéant** is a person who does nothing, an idler.

Faint in "**faint** of heart" means "lacking in courage".

Faith's root is Latin *fides* from *fidere*, "trust".

Faitour is a cheat or imposter.

Fan, as in enthusiast, is an abbreviation of fanatic, from Greek *phanatikos*, "person from the temple"–a god-*intoxicated* person.

Fanatic comes from a Latin word for "pertaining to a temple" or inspired by or frenzied by a god.

A **fanlight** is a semicircular or rectangular window over a door or other window.

Farewell is literally, "go well".

Far-fetched originally meant "brought from far".

A **farl** is a chunk of bread.

To **fastigiate** is to make pointed .

Fastigiated means "sloping up to a point".

Fastuous means haughty, pretentious.

Fatal first meant "decreed by fate".

Fatstock is livestock fattened for slaughter.

Fatuous is derived from Latin *fatuus*, "foolish".

Faucet probably came from French meaning "bore, tap".

Faust is an adjective meaning happy.

Fear first meant "sudden calamity" or "danger".

Someone may be **fearful**; someone or something may be **fearsome**.

Feasible means capable of being done (not probable or plausible).

Featous means well-proportioned or handsome.

February was the month of the festival of purification for the ancient Romans "*Februa*", from Latin *februum*, "purgation".

To **feek** is to wander aimlessly.

To **feer** is to mark off land for plowing.

Fellowfeel is to share the feelings of others, sympathise with.

Male except to be influenced by its spelling; it is a diminutive of *femina*, woman and male comes from latin *masculus*.

Fenugreek literally means "Greek hay" as the Romans used this dried plant for foder.

Feracious means fruitful, prolific.

Festival was for some time an adjective referring to a fest day of the church.

Festive, when said of a person, can mean "fond of feasting".

A decorative chain is a **festoon**.

Fetid is a synonym for stinking.

To **fetishize** is to overvalue.

A **fetlock** is a tuft of hair on a horse's leg.

Feud is from the Gemanic base of foe.

Fey means "fated to die".

Fiancé is French for a "promise".

Fifth-generation means "using artificial intelligence".

Final is from Latin *finis*, "end".

Finance comes from old French *finer* "make an end; settle a debt" and old French *fin* "payment, end" (from Latin *finis*, "end").

Finesse is the clarity or purity of metals.

A **fingerfull** is a pinch or small quantity.

Each of the fingers of a glove is a **fingerling**.

A **fingerpost** is a sign at a road junction with attached signs pointing in the directions of places indicated.

Your lower lip is your **fipple.**

Fireflies are not flies, they are beetles.

First was originally a superlative form "most in front" as it comes from Indo-European *pro* "in front before".

First-foot means "to be the first person to cross someone's threshold in the New Year".

A **firth** is a narrow inlet from the sea.

Fist literally refers to the number of fingers on the hand.

A **fizgig** is a frivolous woman.

The **flashlight** was first called an electric hand torch.

Flaskisable means changeable.

Flat as an apartment (a British usage) comes from an obsolete word *flet*, "floor dwelling" of Germanic origin.

Flathers is a synonym for rubbish or dirt.

Flatulent comes from Latin *flatus*, "blowing, blast".

Flatware is knives, forks, and/or spoons not made of silver.

Flavour first meant fragrance or smell and may be a blend of Latin *flatus*, "blowing, breath" and *foetor*, "stench".

Flerking is jerking or twitching.

Fleshment is excitement from a first success.

A **flexitarian** is one who eats vegetarian at home but who will eat meat or fish in a restaurant or as a guest.

One meaning of **flight** is state of agitation or trembling.

Flinch used to mean "slink, sneak off".

Flippant once meant flexible, nimbles, pliant.

A limb adapted for swimming is a **flipper**—like that of a penguin, seal, or turtle.

Flirt is either imitative of flick or spurt or both words.

To **flob** is to move clumsily or aimlessly.

Flonker is anything very large or outrageous.

Floor goes back to Proto-Germanic floruz "flat surface".

The earliest sense of **floozy** (late 19c-early 20c) is "a girl or young woman" and evolved quickly to one of questionable character.

Florescent refers to a time of blossoming or flowering.

Floss is a word for untwisted filaments of silk used in making embroidery or satin.

A **flummery** is an empty compliment.

A **flump** is a heavy sound of something moving, falling, or dropping heavily.

A **flurch** is a multitude or great many things (not persons).

To **flurn** is to show contempt by looks.

Flurry may be a blend of flutter and hurry.

Flush may be a blend of flash and gush if something is aligned with a margin, it is **flush**.

Fluster first meant "make slightly drunk" fluster and frustrate makes **flustrate**.

Fogdom is a region where nothing is clear, the state of fog.

Folio originally designated the largest size of book.

Format originally pertained to the physical characterstics of a book or other objects—especially the shape on size.

Formication is a sensation of ants creeping over one's skin.

Formulate can mean "reduce to a formula".

Fortunate means good fortune, while **Fortuitous** means merely happening by chance or accident.

A **fosse** is a canal, ditch, or trench and a fossette is a small hollow or depression (as in bone or stell).

Foxfire is the phosphorescent light emitted by decaying timber.

To **frab** is to harass or worry.

A **fractious** person is one whose self-control is easily broken.

Frail first meant "morally weak"; unable to resist temptation.

Frankfurter is short for Frankfurter *wurst*, literally, Frankfurt sausage.

Frankincense is literally frank "high-quality" and incense.

Frazzle may be a blend of fray and *fazle/fasel*, "ravel".

Free goes way back to a base meaning "to love".

Freeganism is obtaining as much of one's food as possible from free sources.

Frequent is from Latin *frequens*, "crowded or regularly repeated".

A **frescade** is a cool shady alley or walkway (*fresco* is Italian for cool, fresh).

A **freshet** is a small stream of fresh water.

Freshman's origin is somewhat obvious, from fresh inexperienced, new.

Fricassee (also fricassée) is (meat) cooked in a white sauce.

Friday is named for Frigg, the ancient Germanic goddess of love.

Fridge is short for the fridgidaire refrigerator; **frig** is a mild curse word.

To **frieze** means to "embroider with gold", to cover with silver, or "to decorate by painting".

A **fritlag** is a worthless man.

Frito means "fried" in Spanish.

A **frittata** (from *fritta,* "freed") is an Italian omelet containing vegetables, cheese, or meat.

Frogging is catching or fishing for frogs.

Frogmarch is walking with your armed pinned behind you.

Fromology is a knowledge of cheeses or the collecting of cheese labels.

To **frot** is to rub or polish.

Frown is from French *froigne*, "surly look"–ultimately of Celtic origin.

Fructose (fruit sugar) is in green plants, fruits, and honey; **glucose** is a simple sugar (also **dextrose**) is a simple sugar in grapes, corn, etc.

Fructuous means producing a great deal of fruit.

Fubbery is another word for cheating or deception.

Fulfil originally meant fill full, fill up.

Fulgent means "dazzlingly bright".

Fulvous means "dull brownish yellow".

Fume comes from Old French *fum*, from Latin *fumus*, "smoke, steam".

Fund's original and literal meaning is "bottom" (Latin *fundus*) but changed to "basic supply, as of money".

Fungology is the science of fungi.

Funicular is literally "running on a rope".

Fundamentalism is now employed to refer to any person or group that is characterised as unbending, rigorous, intolerant, and militant.

Further suggests a removing of obstacles in the way of a desired advance.

Fuzz and **fuzzy** come from German *fussig*, "spongy".

To **fuzzle** is to intoxicate or confuse.

The G in G-string probably stands for "groin"

Gaffe is actually French for "blunder".

Gag was originally an ad-lib joke thrown in by an actor to throw another actor off his lines.

Gaga in French originally meant "senile person".

Comedians are **gagsters.**

A big milk drinker is a **galactophagist**; babies are **galactophagous**.

Galaxy is from Greek *gala, galaktos* "milk" as in Milky Way and galaxy actually means "circle of milk".

The kitchen of a boat, aircraft, or camper is the **galley**.

A man of courage and spirit can be called a **galliard**.

Gallivant may come from French gallant "ladies' man" (from *galer*, "to revel") and avant, "forward".

Galoot first had a nautical use "an inexperienced marine".

Game as a pastime/sport goes back to Germanic meaning "people together, participating".

To **gamel** is to "play games", "frolic".

A **gammerstang** is a tall awkward person.

To **gant** is to "yawn or gape".

Garage is a direct borrowing from French "place where one docks".

Garb first meant "grace, elegance".

Garbanzo is chickpea in Spanish.

Garbology is the anthropological study of a society or culture by examining or analysing its refuse.

Garden may come from Latin *hortus gardinus*, "cultivated plot guarded by a wall" but it is likely to be of Germanic origin and related to "yard".

Gargalesthesia is the feeling caused by tickling.

Garland can figuratively mean "the thing most prized".

Garlic comes from old English *gar*, spear and *leac*, "leek".

Garrulity is talkativeness.

Gash is slang for something extra.

A **gat** is a hole in the ground.

Gaud is a deceitful trick.

A **geek** is any smart person with an obsessive interest, a **nerd** is the same but also lacks social grace, and a **dweeb** is a mega-nerd.

Gaydom is the world of homosexuals.

Geezer first meant "someone who goes around in disguise".

Gelatin is from Italian *gelata*, "jelly".

Genealogy's root is Greek *genea*, "race, generation" and once had the meaning "offspring, progeny".

The word **Genesis** was first the name of the Old Testament book and genetic(s) derive from this word on the pattern of antithetic/antithesis.

A **genicon** is a sexual partner imagined by one who is dissatisfied with his/her actual partner.

Geography is literally "written description of the earth".

A **gerund** is a verb with an-ing ending and which functions as a noun.

Gestapo was an acronym for Geheime Staats Polizie, Hitler's secret police.

Gestation is literally the period during which unborn young are carried inside the womb-from Latin *gerere*, "carry or conduct".

Gesticulate and **gesture** are based on Latin *gerere*, "bear, carry, perform" and **gesticulation** is more exaggerated than a **gesture,** often involving flailing, originally, a person's gesture was their "bearing" or the way they "carried" themselves.

Gesundheit is "health" in German.

Get-go is a nominalisation of the verb phrase to get going "to begin".

Gherkin is from Dutch *gurkkijn*, a diminutive of *gurk*, "cucumber" and it is an immature or small cucumber.

GI is an abbreviation of Government Issue.

Gift first meant "bride price" and was borrowed from Old Norse.

Gignate means to originate or produce.

Ginger, the spice, gives us the figurative use of "mettle" or "spirit".

A **gink** is a person of no consequence.

Gizzard is based on Latin *gigeria*, "cooked entrails of fowl" and it is the strong muscular second stomach of birds in which food is finely ground.

The flat area of the forehead is the **glabella.**

Glacier comes from Latin *glacies*, "ice"; a **Glacialist** studies ice and its impact on geology.

Glam is a word for the loud noise of talking or merrymaking.

Glamour first meant "magic, enchantment" or "art of contriving magic spells".

Glaucoma comes from a Greek word meaning "bluish green or grey," a type of colour haze affecting the eyes; the word was formerly used to denote cataracts.

A person who cuts and fits glass is a **glazier**.

Gleet is sticky, slimy, or greasy filth.

To **gloat** once had the meaning to gaze, stare or to glow (Danish *gloe*).

Glob may be a blend of blob and gob.

Globe, from Latin *globus*, is related to gleba "lump of earth" and etymologically was "something rolled up into a ball".

To be **gloppened** is to be surprised.

A **glory** is a circle of light around the head of a saint or Jesus.

A **glout** is a frown or sullen look.

Glox is the sound of liquid when shaken in a barrel.

Greek *glukus*, "sweet" is the ancestor of **glucose,** the variant *glukeros* was used by a chemist to coin *glycerin/glycerine* for "syrupy liquid".

To **gnap** means to criticise.

Gnathonic means "sycophantic, parasitic".

A **gnomology** is a collection of maxims, sayings, or precepts.

Goat may etymologically be "animal that jumps abouts".

Goblocks are large mouthfuls.

Go-cart first meant "baby walker" as go has an obsolete sense "walk".

Goodish means moderately good.

Goof may have come from the earlier *goff*, an obsolete word meaning "stupid person".

A **goose** has a shorter neck than that of a swan and a shorter, more pointed bill than that of a duck.

Gospel is literally "good news".

Gout is from Latin *gutta*, "drop"—as the disease was believed to be caused by the dropping of diseased matter from the blood into the joints.

Grace is from *gratia*, "pleasure, thanks".

Graciosity is a synonym for graciousness.

Graffiti in Italian is literally "scratches" *graffito* "scratch scribble".

Grain first referred to a single seed of a plant or the pip or stone of a fruit.

Grammar consists of a description of all the elements in a language; **syntax** focuses on the relationships between words that **graft** is the amount of earth that can be dug out in one shoveling of a spade from Old Norse *groftr*, "action of digging" determine that order in the sentences–**grammar** is the entire study and **syntax** is one part only a student of grammar is a **grammatist**.

Grant came through French from Latin *credere*, "believe, trust".

Graphic is from Greek *graphein*, "write" or "scratch".

To **gratulate** is to welcome or greet joyfully.

A strong offensive smell is **graveolence**.

Gravy initially described a spicy sauce.

Gravy now is a soup like addition to meats.

Graze is literally "feed on grass".

Greece was formerly the knee.

Greece was formerly Hellas.

Greed is a back-formation from greedy.

Green is from the same Germanic base **gro-** as grow.

Gremial is an adjective meaning "of or pertaining to the bosom or lap".

Grip is another name for a piece of hand luggage.

Gripe first meant "the action of gripping".

Grizzle can mean "complain, whine".

A **grocer** (literally, "dealer in gross") was originally a wholesaler and the food in retail amounts was called a "spicer"–so a wholesale dealer in these goods was called a "spicer en gross" or "grosser" (from French *gros*, "great, large").

A **grocery** store is smaller; **a supermarket** is big.

Grog was part of a nickname of a Royal Navy admiral who ordered rum rations watered down to curb drunkenness; the nickname came from his coat's material grogram (from French *gros* grain).

Grapple means "to grope" or "to come to grips with".

To **grouk** is to become gradually enlivened after waking.

Groundsel may etymologically mean "ground-swallower".

Grub first referred to root vegetables which had to be grubbed (dug) out of the ground.

Gruesome is from an earlier verb grue, "be terrified".

Guard first meant "care, keeping".

Gubernation is the act of controlling or governing.

Gubernatorial and **governor** trace back to Latin *gubernare*, "to govern" but governor took a detour through French (*governeor*).

Guerrilla is from a Spanish diminutive of *Guerra* war and refers to a soldier of an independent armed resistance force.

Gorilla is the ape.

Gulf comes from Greek *kolphos*, "bosom".

Gullet is from Latin *gula*, throat.

Gunny, the material used for sacks, is made from jute (from Sanskrit *gani*, "sack").

To **guttle** is to eat gluttonously, voraciaoulsy .

Guttural is from Latin *guttur*, "throat".

Gymnasium was a school where Greek youths were given athletic training while naked (*gymnos*).

Gynaecology is from the Greek word for "woman", *gune*.

> **H** is a Roman numeral for 200, B for 300, G or P for 400, and D for 500

Hangout originally meant a place of business—from the signs "hung out" by artisans, professionals, and tradespeople.

Hanky-panky may be an alteration of hokey-pokey.

Haphazard is redundant, with both components meaning "chance".

Hapless means one is lacking hap "good fortune, luck"; the words happy and happiness also have the root "hap".

Haptic means pertaining to the sense of touch.

Hardiment is a word for boldness, courage, or daring.

Harm's original meanings were "grief" before "physical damage".

A **hasp** is a piece of hardware used to lock a door or gate; it fits over a staple or loop and a padlock through that secures the door or gate.

A **harridan** is an ill-tempered, scolding woman.

Hassle may be a blend of haggle and tussle.

Hate means to "dislike intensely, loathe" and **despise** means "look down on contemptuously".

Haul originally had the nautical meaning of "to trim the sails to sail closer to the wind".

Hazard started as the name of a game dice but later extended to all kinds of risks and comes from Arabic *az-zohr*, "gaming die".

Haze is probably a back-formation from hazy.

HAZMAT stands for Hazardous Material.

He ultimately comes from Indo-European ki-/ko- "this, here"—as opposed to "that, there".

A ship's bathroom is the **head**.

Hearse was once the decorative bier, frame, or stand on which a corpse was laid, or a framework to carry candles over a coffin.

Heartburn has on old meaning of "jealousy" or "hatred".

The **hearth** is the floor of a fireplace and the area in front of a fireplace.

The **dent** at the end of your sternum is the **heart-spoon**.

Hebephrenic describes the condition of adolescent silliness.

Hectic was originally a medical term for a type of fever.

Heirloom is a combination of heir and loom "tool, utensil" and it describes any personal property that has been in a family for several generations.

Helicopter comes from Greek *helika*, "screw" and *pteron*, "wing".

"**Hello**," which was an exclamation of surprise dating back to the Middle Ages, from French *hallow*, "to pursue by shouting," first becoming "hallo" in English.

Hepatic (pertaining to or affecting the liver) is from Greek *hepatikos*, "of the liver," and **Hepatitis** is *hepatos*, "liver" and *-itis*, "inflammation".

Latin *heres*, "**heir**" gives us **hereditary**, **heir**, **heritage**, and more.

Hermit is from Greek *eremites*, "solitary"; a **hermitage** (pronounced HUR-muh-tij) is a place where a **hermit** or monks live.

Heroin (the drug) is based on Latin/Greek *heros*, "hero" because of its effects on the user's self-esteem; **heroine** is a courageous principal female character (the counterpart of hero).

Hestern or **hesternal** means "pertaining to yesterday".

Heyday originally was an exclamation expressing excitement, happiness, surprise, or exuberance—and is from Saxon *heh-doeg*, "high day".

Hiccup was originally called a **yex**.

Hiemal means "pertaining to winter; wintry".

Highfalutin actually has no apostrophe; its variant is highfaluting and its origin is unknown.

Hilarious comes from Greek *hilaros*, "cheerful".

The outdoor equivalent of cabin fever is '**hill-nutty**.

Hip-hop is a culture and **rap** is a style of music that is one of the components of **hip-hop**; **hip-hop** music is not the same as **rap**- it is a fusion of rapping and deejaying.

Hippodrome "race track" is from Greek hippo, "horse" and dromos, "running".

armpit hair can be referred to as **hirci**.

Hobble is of Germanic origin, having to do with rocking from side to side; the noun can mean "an awkward situation".

Hoax is probably a contraction of hocus.

A male ferret is a **hob**.

A **hobo** is a migratory worker who likes to travel, a **tramp** travels without working, and a **bum** does not travel or work.

Hocus-pocus is a corruption of the sacred phrase *hoc est corpus meum*, "this is my body," used in the Eucharist.

Hogwash from earlier hoggy swasch, is pig slops, swill of a kitchen or brewery given to hogs.

Homage (pronounced AH-mij) is worshipful reverence or veneration.

The **honda** is the eye at the end of a lasso or lariat through which the rope passes to form a loop.

Honest comes from Latin *honor/honos*, "honour".

Honeymoon implied that everything was sweet after the wedding but, like a full moon, wanes with time; it later came to mean the first month after the wedding.

Hopefully is really supposed to be used for "in a hopeful manner".

Horoscope comes from Greek *hora*, "hour, time" and skopos, "observer".

Horripilating is getting goosebumps from the cold.

Horseplay originally was a play in which a horse was used or took part—or theatrical horsemanship.

Hotchpotch/hodgepodge is an alteration of the earlier hotchpot, borrowed from Old French *Hocher*, "shake" and *pot*, "pot" ("shake the pot").

HOV stands for high-occupancy vehicle.

A conical building enclosing a kiln is a **hovel**.

Howdy is a shortened form of "How do you do?".

Hub first meant "a shelf at the side of a fireplace used for heating pans".

Hubris is Greek, literally "insolence".

Hue and cry is somewhat redundant as **hue** means "short, make an outery"; **hue** and **cry** was a medieval law requiring that all citizens within earshot– give chase to a fleeing criminal.

Hug is probably of Scandinavian origin— tracing to words meaning "comfort, console" and "affection".

Humiliate is from Latin *humilis*, "humble".

Hummacky means "having an uneven surface".

Hurdle refers to a difficulty or obstacle; **hurtle** means to move with great speed and violence.

Hurly-burly is turmoil or an uproar.

Hurrah hurray, and **hooray** are alterations of **huzza**, a *sailor's* cheer.

Husband comes from the German words *hus* and *bundo*, meaning "houseowner" and originally had nothing to do with marital status; in Old English, **husband** was literally "housebound" —bound to the house and family.

The word **hussy** is just a corruption of "housewife" and originally had no unkind implications and for many years was not applied to a married woman.

Hydraulic comes from Greek *hydor*, "water" and *aulos*, "pipe".

Hydroponics comes from combining *hydro-* with *ponos*, "labour" and is patterned on geoponics; **hydroponics** is also known as aquaculture or tank farming.

A **hydropot** is a water drinker and a **galactophagist** is a milk drinker.

A **hyperdisyllable** is a word of more than two syllables.

Difficulty in making decisions is **hypobulia**.

Hyponoia is hidden meaning or significance.

A vague feeling of sadness, seemingly without cause is **hypophrenia** and a vague feeling of mental discomfort is **malnoia**.

Hyposomnia is another way of saying lack of sleep.

Profound melancholy can be called **hypothimia**.

I is from an Indo-European root shared by Latin and Greek "ego"

Iatrapistia is a lack of faith in doctors or medicine and **iatromisia** is a dislike of doctors.

Ichabod is an exclamation of lament for the good old days.

Ichnography is a floor plan for a building. The **ichthus** is the fish image used as a Christian symbol.

An **icon** was originally a "simile" in rhetoric and the etymological idea of **icon** is of "similarity," from Greek *eikon*, "likeness, similarity".

ID is preferred over I.D. as the abbreviation for identification.

Idem is the Latin word for ditto.

Another name for a trademark is an **idiograph**.

Ignore is properly used of things that are present in our surroundings; but for things like rules, conventions, stipulations, contracts, the right word is **disregard**.

Ignore and **ignorant** are from Latin *i-*, "not" and *gno-*, "know".

Illapse is a gradual advance.

Literally, **illegitimate** is "not lawful" and **illicit** is "not allowed".

Illeism is the practice of referring to one-self in the third person.

Illth is the opposite of wealth.

Illusion is based on a Latin word meaning "jest, mock, play".

Imago is the final, fully developed adult insect stage.

Imbecile, from Latin *imbecillus*, "without stick, staff" was someone without a crutch to lean on, and first meant "physically weak".

Imbibe once had the meaning "to admit into the mind"; the corresponding noun for **imbibe** is **imbibitions**.

Immaculate comes from Latin words meaning "not stained".

Immediate is from Latin meaning "not intervening" and the first sense was "nearest in space or order".

Immote is a word meaning "unmoved".

Impart first meant "give a share of".

Impatient is from Latin (*pati*, "to suffer") meaning "not able to bear or suffer".

Hinder or prevent was an early sense of **impeach**.

Impede is from Latin *impedire*, "shackle the feet of".

Impertinent first meant "not belonging (to); unrelated, unconnected" and eventually it came to mean "behaving without proper respect; presumptuous, intrusive".

Implacable means "irreconcilable" and "unable to be appeased".

Impletion is "filling up, making full" or the condition of being filled.

Implicate first meant "entangle, intertwine" and is based on Latin *plicare*, "to fold" and a person implicated for a crime is "wrapped up" in it somehow; **implication** is the noun corresponding to both **implicate** and imply.

Import first meant "carry, cause, convey".

A product from abroad is an **import**; the process is **importation**.

Important and import come from Latin *importare* (*in-* and *portare*, "carry").

Impresario comes from the Italian word *impresa*, "undertaking".

Impress stresses the depth and persistence of the effect.

An **imprest** is a monetary advance, from the obsolete verb **imprest** "to lend".

To **imprint** is to cause a young animal to accept its parent as the proper object of affection; the learning process of young animals is called **imprinting**.

Impromptu is based on Latin *in promptu*, "in readiness" from *promptus*, "prepared, ready".

Improve first meant "to make a profit for oneself" or "to employ to advantage; to make profitable use of".

Inane, from Latin *inonis*, first meant "empty" words meaning "babbling, full of idle talk"; include **inaniloquent** and **inaniloquous**.

Inapt is "not suitable or appropriate" while **unapt** is "not likely or inclined".

Inaugurate is from Latin *inauguruat-*, "interpreted as omens (from the flight of birds)"—from *augurare* "to auger".

Incense once meant to kindle any passion, good or bad.

Inch-meal means gradually or by inches or small degrees.

The base of **incinerate** is Latin *ciner-*, "ashes" an **incipient** is a beginner.

Incognito is Italian "unknown, disguised," from Latin *incognitus*, "unknown".

Income originally meant "arrival, entrance"; a place of entrance can be called an **incoming**.

Incredible means "unbelievable" and **incredulous** means "unbelieving".

Indagatrix is a female searcher or investigator.

Induce can mean "derive by reasoning from facts"; the base of **induce** and **induction** is Latin *ducere*, "to lead".

Indict (to accuse or formally charge) was first spelled endite or indite.

Indolent means "habitually lazy".

Indulge came from Latin *indulgere*, "allow long enough for".

Ineluctable means "inescapable; that cannot be struggled out of".

Inequity is "injustice, unfairness"; **iniquity** refers to "immorality, sin, wickedness".

Inermous means "without thorns or prickles".

Inert is literally, "having no art or skill".

Infantry was originally applied to soldiers who were too young to serve in the cavalry.

Infatuate is based on Latin elements meaning "make foolish".

Influenza is Italian for "influence" because the disease was thought to be influenced by the stars.

Infringe first meant "break down, destroy".

Injure and **injury** come from Latin *in-* against" and *Ius/Iur*, "right," i.e., wrongful action or treatment; **injure** is a back formation from **injury**.

To **inkle** is to communicate in an undertone or whisper, to give a hint of something, which gives us **inkling**.

The word **innate** means "inborn" and should apply to living things; **inherent** is "essential, intrinsic" and applies best to non-living things like ideas.

Innocent is *in-*, "free from" and *nocere*, "hurt, injure" (Latin).

Innocuous is "harmless, not hurtful," from Latin *in-*, "not" and *nocere*, "to hurt".

Inseminate is derived from Latin *seminare*, "to sow, to plant".

Insight is literally, internal sight or mental vision.

Insipid means tasteless or having only a slight taste.

Insist "to dwell at length (on or in)" is from Latin *sistere* "stand".

Inspire comes from Latin meaning "breathe or blow into," its literal original sense.

Insulin gets its name from the body part called islets of Langerhans, from which the hormone involved is produced.

Insult first meant "to leap on the prostrate body of a foe" or "attack or attacking," especially a surprise military assault, and the word comes from the Latin base of *saltus*, "leap".

Insure and **ensure** mean "to make certain" but only **insure** can mean "indemnify against loss".

Intelligent is from Latin *inter-*, and *legere*, "gather, pick up, read".

Intend had an early meaning "to stretch out, extend, intensify".

Interim is from a Latin word meaning "meanwhile".

Interior is Latin, literally "inner".

Internet should be capitalized, but **intranet** should be lowercase; **Internet** was coined from inter (national) + (Arpa) net.

Intestate is from Latin *in-*, "not" and *testatus*, "testified" and the word refers to having made no legally valid will before death.

Intestine as an adjective can mean "domestic, taking place within a nation".

Latin *intoxicore* meant "to poison" as Greek soldiers dipped their arrows in *toxicum*, "poison"—later giving us **intoxicate**.

Intrepid is based on Latin *trepidus*, "alarmed".

Introduce means literally "lead inside" from Latin *introducere*, "lead in".

Intropunitive means "blaming oneself rather than others or external events".

Inuit is the plural of *inuk* "person".

Inunction is the rubbing of oil or lotion into the skin.

Invite comes from Latin *invitare*, from an Indo-European root meaning "to go after something, pursue with vigour, desire".

Inwit is the conscience or wisdom and **outwit** is acquired knowledge or information.

ISBN stands for International Standard Book Number and each book has a unique one.

Islamania is a passion for islands.

Words that don't repeat any letters are known as **isograms**.

Isometric is from Latin *isus*, "equal" and *metria*, "measuring".

Issue and **exit** are closely related, going back to Latin *exire* "go out," which became Old French *eissue* and later **issue**, and Latin *exitus* and then exit.

Isuzu means "50 bells" in Japanese.

The name of the letter Z is **izzard**.

> **J** was formerly interchangeable with I and up to a point the two were not separated in English dictionaries, alphabetical lists, etcetera

Jacent means "lying, recumbent"—so **adjacent** means "lying next to".

A **jackleg** is a reckless driver.

Jaded originally referred to a "worn-out" horse.

January is named for Janus, the Roman god of gates and doors and beginnings, who had two faces—one looking forward to the future and one looking backward to the past.

Jargogle means "to confuse, to mix up".

The original sense of **jargon** was "chattering, twittering," and then "gibberish"—coming from French *jargoun*, "warbling of birds".

Jaundice is based on French *jaune*, "yellow".

Jazz can mean "energy, excitement".

A **jazzbo** is a jazz musician.

Jeans are made of cloth that was originally called Gene fustian or Geane, the name for Genoa, Italy, in Middle English; **jeannette** is any fabric resembling jean.

Jest first meant "exploit, heroic deed" and then "a story of heroic deeds"—from Latin *gesta,* "exploits, actions".

Jesus means "anointed one" and Buddha means "the Enlightened".

Jewel may be from French *Jeu*, "play," and some say from Latin *jocus*, "jest".

Jiffy is an actual unit of time—.01 second.

A **jilt** is a woman accomplice to a thief.

The gold circles on a tambourine's edge are the **jingles**.

Joinhand is an old name for cursive writing.

A **joist** is a parallel timber to which floor boards or ceiling laths are fastened. Latin *locus*, "jest, joke" gave us **joke**.

Jolly comes from Old French *jolif*, "merry, festive, pleasant".

Journey's first sense was a day's (*jour*) travel.

Judge is from Latin jus, "law," and *dicere*, "to say".

Judicial means "pertaining to judges or the courts" and **judicious** means "prudent, carefully considered"; **judicial** refers to judgement as it is exercised by the court, **judicious** is judgement as it is exercised by an individual.

Juggle is from Latin *joculus*, a diminutive of jocus, "jest," and a **juggler** was originally a jester.

July and **August** were originally named, respectively, Quintilis (fifth) and Sextilis (sixth) month; September is septem, "seven," November novem, "nine," and December decem, "ten"; both **July** and **August** are named for Roman Empire leaders: Julius Caesar and Augustus Caesar.

Jumbo originally denoted a large and clumsy person and the word may come from Swahili *jambe*, "chief".

June is either named for Juno, the queen of the Roman gods and the goddess of marriage—or named for Junius, a prominent ancient Roman family.

The art of taking photographs of people jumping, in order to capture their essence and also for scientific study, is **jumpology**.

Juventude is another word for "youth".

> **K** for strike-out in baseball comes from the last letter of "struck"

Kalon is the kind of beauty that is more than skin deep.

Kaput was originally a card game term for "being without tricks" in the game piquet.

Karaoke means "empty orchestra" in Japanese.

Karoshi is death caused by overwork.

Kedogenous is "brought about by worry or anxiety".

keister first meant "suitcase" or "satchel".

To **kelk** is to groan or belch.

Kempt means "combed" or "neatly kept".

Kerosene is based on Greek *keros*, "wax".

Khaki comes from Persian *khak*, "dust, earth".

Kid originally denoted a young goat.

Kindergarten is German for "children's garden"—a term for a school in which children's aptitude for learning is cultivated.

A **kine** is an isolated body movement or gesture.

Kinemics is the study of gestures as units of expression.

Kinesics and *pasimology* are other terms for body language.

Kitty (now pool of money) may be from the slang meaning "jail".

Knabble means to bite or nibble.

Knickknack has two k's in the middle.

Know is from an Indo-European root shared by Latin (*g*)*noscere* and Greek *gignoskein*.

Knowledge is the information held on a computer system; the word was originally a verb meaning "acknowledge, recognize".

Kowtow comes from Chinese kou tou, "knock one's head" which would occur during prostration out of respect, worship, etc.

Kudos is best pronounced KYOO-dahs or KYOO-dohs and derives from Greek kydos, "glory, praise, renown"; in Greek, it means a single bit of praise or prestige, but the word looks like an English plural and is therefore treated as one.

A **kyle** is a narrow sea channel between two islands (from Scottish).

> **L**, V, X, and D as Roman numerals are not abbreviations for Latin words but rather may commemorate primitive Roman symbols

Labefaction is a deterioration or downfall.

Label originally meaning "narrow band or strip", and comes from a French word meaning "ribbon".

The word for "the ability to read lips" is **labiomancy**.

Lackadaisical comes from an old term **lackaday**, which means "Shame on you, day" as if it were a person.

Laclabphily is said to be the collecting of cheese labels.

Lad meant "servant" before it acquired a more general sense of "youth".

Lady is from Old English *hlaf*, "loaf" and a Germanic base meaning "knead" and first literally meant "one who kneads bread".

Lair first meant "grave, tomb" or "place where one sleeps".

Lake first meant pool or pond.

Landscape comes from Dutch *landschap*, "region, tract of land".

Language is from Latin *lingua*.

Languor is any distressed condition, such as illness, sorrow, fatigue, etc.

Lapidary first meant "pertaining to stones".

To **lapidate** is to pelt someone with stones.

Lappet is a fold or hanging piece of flesh in some animals.

Larceny comes from *larcin*, the French word for mercenary soldier—as they were expected to indulge in petty theft.

Lascivious means "inclined to lust".

Laser is an acronym for Light Amplification by Stimulated Emission of Radiation.

Lassitude is mental weariness.

Late comes from Indo-European *lad*, "slow, weary" which begat Latin *lassus*, "tired" before English late "slow".

Latent means "hidden, concealed" and its opposite is patent.

Latescent means "becoming obscure or hidden away".

A **laud** is a hymn of praise.

Laudable means deserving praise; **Laudatory** means expressing praise.

Laundry comes from Latin *lavare*, "wash"—as does lavatory, which first meant "place or vessel for washing".

Lavender got its name from the custom of adding it to the laundry and baths (Latin *lavare*, "to wash"); lavender once meant "laundress".

Lavish traces back to French *lavache*, "deluge of rain".

Lawn comes from laund, "a glade or pasture".

A **layette** is a set of clothing, accessories, and equipment for a new baby

One meaning of **leave** is "approval, pleasure".

A **lectern** is the stand on which the speaker's notes are placed, the **podium** is the platform on which the speaker and **lectern** stand, a **platform** for several people is a **dais**, and a **rostrum** is a platform for one or more.

The finger next to the little finger is the **leech-finger**.

Leek is from German and forms the second syllable of garlic.

Leg-of-mutton sleeves means that they resemble a leg of mutton, very full and loose on the arm but close-fitting at the wrist.

Lens is from Latin for "*lentil*" because of the similarity in shape.

Lesson etymologically, is "something read," from Latin *lectio*, "reading" from legere, "read"—so lesson is literally the action of reading to oneself.

Lethonomia is the inability to recall the right name.

Letter is from Latin *littera*, "alphabetic symbol" or, in the plural, "document".

Leukemia is from Greek *leukas*, "white" and *emia* (from *haima*) "blood".

Leviathan is Hebrew for a sea monster which can only be subdued by God, so it came to mean a very large or powerful thing.

Level is based on Latin *labella*, diminutive of *librs*, balance, scales.

Lexicography is the art of defining words or compiling lexicons.

A dictionary and wordbook collector is a **lexiconophilist**.

Libberwort is food or drink that makes one idle and stupid, food of no nutritional value, i.e., junk food.

Libertine first meant freedman or son of a freedman.

Licit means not forbidden by law; allowable the opposite of illicit.

Lieu instead is from Middle English via French from Latin *locus*, place.

Lightsome can mean not weighed down by cares.

Light-time is the time required for light to travel from a distant object to Earth.

Lilt comes from a word meaning pipe and the noun originally meant song, tune.

Limaceous means slug-like or pertaining to slugs.

Linden is another name for a lime tree.

Lingo traces back to Latin *lingua*, tongue if someone is **linguacious**, they are talkative.

Lip comes from Latin *labrum*, lip.

Lip-clap is kissing.

Liquor (from Latin), though the words have different meanings—**liqueur** is a strong highly flavoured, often sweetened, alcoholic beverage made by distillation rather than fermentation (which would be beer, wine).

List as in catalogue comes from French *liste*, band, border or strip of paper, catalogue, from Proto-Germanic *liston*; the sense of enumeration is from strips of paper used as a sort of catalogue.

Listen is from the Indo-European base *klu-*, hearing.

Literally means actually or to the letter.

Littlemeal means little by little.

Live (adjective) is a shortening of alive.

Liveware refers to working personnel, as opposed to abstract or inanimate things they work with.

Lob comes from an old noun meaning lout or pendulous object.

Lobe (as in ear) is from Greek *lobos*, "something round".

Logarithm is from Greek *logos*, "reckoning, ratio and arithmos, number".

A **logion** is a traditional saying or proverb of a sage.

Logo is an abbreviation or logogram or logotype.

Logology is the pursuit of word puzzles; also the science of words.

Loiter may come from Middle Dutch *loteren*, "wag about".

Longevity is from Latin *longus*, "long", and *aevum*, "age", literally "long life".

Loo is probably a fanciful form of French *l'eau*, the water.

Lorate means shaped like a strap.

A **lorimer** is a saddle-maker.

To **lout** is to treat with contempt.

Louvre comes from French *lovier*, skylight and was first a domed turret-like part of a roof for smoke to leave or light to come in.

Love in tennis comes from *l'oeuf*, "egg" as a zero looks like an egg; we sometimes call zero a "goose egg".

Lubricous means slippery (literally or figuratively).

Lugubrious means mournful, sorrowful payment of ransom is luition.

Lunacy is insanity, once believed to be brought on by changes in the moon.

Lunatic can mean influenced by the moon.

Lunch comes from Scottish *lonch*, a "hunk of meat" and it first meant hunk, thick piece, a large piece of anything, especially edible like bread or cheese.

Luscious may be an alteration of obsolete **licious**, a shortened form of delicious.

Lusk means lazy or sluggish.

Lusory is used as a pastime or playful.

Lutose means covered with mud.

Lycanthropy is a type of insanity in which the patient imagines himself as a beast.

> Like **B** and **P**, **M** is in the category of consonants called labials, from Latin for "lip". Labials are formed with no need of teeth or tricky tongue movement

Macarism is pleasure in another's happiness.

A **macher** is a person who gets things done.

Macilent means "lean, thin or shrivelled", i.e., lacking in substance.

Macrology is long and tiresome talk.

Madam is French, literally, "my lady".

Magenta is named for a town in Italy that was the site of a battle shortly before the dye was discovered.

Magniloquence refers to a language that is lofty and extravagant, whereas. **Grandiloquence** refers to a language that is pompous or bombastic.

Magnitude first meant "greatness of character".

A **mainpast** is a person's household or a household servant.

Malaise comes from French words translating to "bad, ill and ease".

Maledicent means addicted to abusive speech.

Malic means having to do with apples.

Mall first meant a mallet used in a game, the game itself, and also the alley in which the game was played, giving rise to its meaning as "a sheltered area".

Malmy pertains to weather that is warm and sticky; **malnoia** is a vague feeling of mental discomfort.

Manage first meant to handle or train a horse and it is based on Latin *manus*, "hand".

Manducate means to chew or eat.

Mania is based on a Greek word meaning "madness", ultimately from an Indo-European root for mind.

Manicure is from Latin *manus*, hand, and *cura* care.

Manky means bad, inferior, or worthless.

A **manling** is a little man or dwarf.

Manumit means "set free", Latin literally "send" out from one's "hand".

Map comes from Latin *mappa mundi*, "sheet of the world" from *mappa*, napkin, tablecloth.

Marathon, from the town in Greece, gets its meaning from the distance a messenger ran, carrying news of a victory over the Persians in 499 BC.

The game of **marbles** originally used balls made of marble.

Maritime is from Latin *mare*, sea and *timusm* near, neighbouring.

A **mark** was originally a boundary, frontier or limit.

Market is from Old Provencal *mercari*, by, and the word originally denoted "a place where people met to trade goods" (from Latin *mercatus*); **mart** is a variant.

Marmalade comes from Portuguese *marmelada* "quince" jam, from Latin *melomeli*, "honey flavoured with quinces, and *melimela*, sweet apple.

Mascara comes from an Italian word for mask.

Mascot is from Provencal *masco*, sorcerer, witch a person or thing that is supposed to bring good luck.

Massage probably comes from Arabic *massa*, "to feel, handle, palpate".

Master is from Latin *magister*, "chief".

Masticate is from Greek *mastikhan*, "gnash" or "grind the teeth".

Mathematical is base on Greek, *mathema*, science, from manthanein, "learn mathematic(s)" first referred to" something learned".

Matinee, literally French for morning, is so called because these performances once took place in the morning.

Matins is a morning church service or the first mass of the day.

Matriculation is formal admission to a college or university and is based on Latin matricula, register, catalog.

Matrimony is from Latin *matrimonium*, state of being married, from *mater*, "mother", and *monium, mony* (state, condition).

Matter is from Latin material, "timber" or "stuff of which something is made or subject of discourse".

Mattoid means semi-nuts or behaving erratically.

Mattress comes from Arabic al-*matrah*, "bed, carpet, cushion, seat".

Maudlin is a corruption of Magdalene, the woman who weeped at the feet of Jesus as he was crucified.

Maundy descends from a Latin word meaning commandment, so **Maundy** Thursday refers to the mandate given by Jesus at the Last Supper.

Mayor's ancestor is Latin *maior*, "person in authority", from *maior*, "greater".

Meat first meant food, nourishment especially solid food as opposed to drink.

A **meatus** is a channel or passage.

Mediocre is from Latin *mediocris*, of "middle height" or degree from Latin *medius, mid*, and *ocris*, "rugged mountain".

Medicine's Indo-European root is "measure" and literally means "the science of taking appropriate measures concerning one's heath."

Melancholy comes from Greek *melan* black, and *cholos*, bile as black bile caused a sorrowful feeling.

Melodrama's origin is Greek (*melos*, "music, song") meaning "song play" and it started out as a sensational play interspersed with songs.

Melody is from Greek *melos*, "song" and an early sense was "sweet music".

Mend is a shortening of amend.

A **merenda** is a light meal.

Meridian's root is Latin *meridianum*, "midday".

Mermaid is from *mere*, "sea" and "maid".

Messuage is a house, its outbuildings, and the adjacent land.

Mete, the verb "first meant" measure the dimensions or quantity–**meter** was first person who measures (from Greek *metron*).

Meteor (Greek raised up, lofty) was first applied to any atmospheric phenomenon, e.g., watery (aqueous) meteors were precipitation such as rain, snow, hail, etc. which is where **Meteorology** gets its name.

Metopic means "pertaining to the forehead".

Metrology is the science of measurement.

A young grandmother is a **metrona**.

Microbiology specialises in microbes (Greek "small life") microorgainsims commonly called germs.

Micrology is the investigation and classification of trivial matters.

Microsoft is an abbreviation of microcomputer software.

Mien is from Chinese for "wheat flour" and these are wheat flour noodles used in dishes like lo mein, chow mein (note change of spelling).

If someone is in a **miff,** they are in a fit of pique or a huff.

Milieu is from Latin *medius*, "mid", and *lieu*, "place".

Minaret derives from Turkish *minaret*, "lighthouse, tall tower".

Mindshare is the consumer awareness of a brand or product.

Minikin refers to a petite or dainty person.

Minimize means to reduce to an absolute minimum–not to play down or soften.

Minister was originally a person acting under the authority or as an agent of another.

Mint as in money comes from Latin *moneta*.

Minuscule comes from medieval manuscript writing, literally, *minscula littera,* "somewhat smaller letter."

A **misnancy** is an effeminate character.

A **misologist** is one who is averse to conflict, but a **misologist** may also be one who does not want to discuss something but prefers to plunge ahead.

A person who cannot stand learning is a **misomusist**.

Miss is a shortened form of mistress.

A **mittimus** is an official order sending someone to prison.

Mizle means to "lead astray, to deceive".

Mizmaze is confusion or bewilderment.

Fine or light rain or drizzle can be called **mizzle**.

Mnemotechnics is another name for memory techniques.

Mob is from Latin *mobile vulgus*, which meant "the masses" or "disorderly crowd".

Modest comes from Latin modestus, "keeping due measure".

A napkin tucked in a collar to protect clothes is a **mokador** or **bib**.

Molest first meant "cause trouble to" or "annoy, vex".

Money comes from *moneta*, a Latin word that was an epithet of the goddess Juno, in whose temple a mint was housed.

Latin **momentum**, from *movere*, "move" and *mentum*, is the source of **moment**, which first meant moving power and is obviously the source of **momentum**.

Monday is "day of the Moon", a translation of *lunas dies* (Latin).

Monochrome's original meaning is different shades of one colour.

Monocle, a one-lense eyeglass, once meant "one-eyed".

Monopoly is made up of *mono* plus Greek *polein*, sell.

Monops means "having one eye".

Moonwalk was coined in 1969, the year of the first moon landing.

Morbid first meant "indicative of disease".

Morgue is from French and was originally the name of a Paris building where dead bodies were kept until identified.

Morphology is the study of the form of words in a language, including change, formation and inflection; the word **morphology** contains the root *log*- "study", and it first referred to the study of biological forms.

Mortuary was originally a gift claimed by a parish priest from a dead person's estate.

A **mount** is a conical hill of moderate height.

Moustache comes via French from Italian *mostaccio*, which goes back to Greek *mustax*, "upper lip, **moustache**".

Mug the verb, first meant "to strike in" or "strangle"; a **muggee** is a victim of a mugging.

A **mullet** is a hairstyle that is short in front and on the sides, long at the back.

Mulligatawny is from Tamil *milagu-tannir*, "pepper water," which partially describes the highly seasoned soup.

Munch is imitative of crunch and scrunch.

Mung is a crowd of people.

Mungency is nose noise.

Municipal's history includes Latin *municeps*, "citizen with privileges," from *munia*, "civic offices".

Murphy is slang for potato.

Mushroom and **mush** are slang for "umbrella".

Mutual applies to reciprocal relationships between two or more things; if something is held in **common**, use "**common**" instead.

Myth is from Greek *mythos*, "a fable, "a story, or tale".

Mythopoeic means "creating or giving rise to a myth or myths".

> You need your nose to pronounce **N**. **N** and **M** are the only nasal sounds in English. **N** is basically three-quarters of an **M**'s shape.

Nadir (pronounced NAY-dur) is the point directly under your feet.

Name is ancient and goes back to Indo-European *nomen*, then Latin *nomen*, and Greek-*onoma*.

To **name-check** is to mention or acknowledge by name.

Napalm is the compound naphthemic palmitate.

The nasty-smelling mothball substance is **naphthalene**.

Narcotic is from Greek *narkoun*, "make numb".

A **natkin** is a disagreeable taste or smell.

Naupathia is seasickness.

Neat as in "clean, clear" comes from Latin *nidus* "shining, clean"; **neat** first meant "free from impurities".

A **nebula** is a dust cloud in outer space.

Neck oiginally was just the back portion of the body connecting the head and shoulders.

Needle has the same Indo-European base as Latin *nere*, "to spin," and Greek *nema*, "thread".

Neighbour is Germanic *neigh/neah*, "near", and "*gebur*", dweller.

Neoteny is the prolongation of the period of immaturity.

Nerve comes from Latin *nevus*, "sinews, bowstring".

Net as in "without deductions" came from French *net* as "neat" and then evolved to *net* "free from any (further) deduction".

Netop is a synonym for friend.

News first meant "new things, novelties".

Niche is from Old French *ninchier*, "make a nest".

Nickname is from a misdivision of "an eke-name" (*eke* meaning "addition") into "neke-name".

Nifty is a name for a joke or witty remark.

Night-shine is a term for faint light perceptible at night.

Nikhedonia is the pleasure derived from anticipating success.

Ninny-broth was another name for coffee.

A nip is one fourth of a bottle or a half-pint (of ale, especially), a **baby** is one eighth of a bottle of wine.

Nitwit comes from Dutch *niet wit*, "I don't know".

A **nob** is a person of elegance and high social standing.

Noctidial means "lasting for or comprising of a night and a day".

A **noddary** is a foolish act.

A **noggin** is another name for mug or cup.

To **noggle** is to walk awkwardly.

Noise first meant quarreling and comes from Latin *nausea*, "feeling of disgust".

Noisome means "evil-smelling, offensive" and it comes from "*noy*", a shortened form of annoy.

Nomad comes from the base of Greek *nemein*, "to pasture".

Nominate means call the name of (Latin *nomen*), while **denominate** means to give a name to.

Nonchalant comes from French *nonchaloir*, "not heated", ultimately from Latin *noncalere*, "not warm or aroused".

Noology is the science of intuition and reason as phenomena of the mind.

Noon is derived from the Latin word for "ninth" as it originally meant the ninth hour after sunrise, about 3 PM.

Neither **noon** nor **midnight** is 12 a.m. or 12 p.m. because neither comes before or after the moment the sun is on the meridian.

Nor is a contraction of Old English *nother*, "neither".

The **nose-piece** is the part of eyeglasses that rest on the nose.

A **nosology** is a classification or list of diseases.

Nostalgia comes from Greek *nostos*, "homeward journey, return home" and "*algos*", pain—the word *nostos* originally referring to the journey of Odysseus and the heroes from Troy.

Nostril comes from Old English words meaning "nose hole".

Notary is from Latin *notarlus*, "shorthand writer or clerk".

A **notelet** is a short note or notecard.

Notify first meant "take note of, notice, observe".

Nourish first meant "bring up, or rear (a child or animal)".

Nova was originally a new star or *nebula* Italian *novella storia*, "new story" begat "**novel**".

Noxious comes from Latin *noxius*, "harmful".

Nubile etymologically means "suitable for marriage," from Latin *nubere*, "take a husband".

Nucal means pertaining to nuts.

Number is regularly used with count nouns, while **amount** is mainly used with mass nouns: **number** of mistakes, **amount** of money.

Numeracy is having arithmetic skills (like literacy for reading).

Nuncheon was the first name for lunch, from *noon schenche* (drink)—a drink taken at noon.

Nyctalopia is poor vision in low light.

Nylon is an invented word patterned on "cotton" and "rayon".

O is the oldest letter of the English alphabet.

One who is **obdurate** is stubbornly impenitent.

Obese is from Latin *obesus*, literally "having eaten oneself fat".

Oblique can mean "indirect," as in a course or expression.

A meaning of **obliterate** is to cancel a postage stamp.

Obnoxious first meant "subject or liable to harm or injury" (Latin *ob-*, "toward," and *noxa*, "harm, injury").

Obscene comes from Latin *obscenus*, "ill-omened" or "indecent".

Obtain can mean "prevail, succeed, win".

The **occiput** is the back of the head (Latin *ob*. and *caput*, "head").

The **occident** is the region of the sky where the sun sets—the west (the opposite of **Orient**, the east).

Occult first meant "hidden from sight; concealed" (Latin *ob-*, and *celare*, "conceal").

Occupy's Latin root is *ob-*, "over," and *capere*, "seize, take".

Occur comes from Latin *occurrere*, "run to meet".

O'clock is an abbreviation for "of the clock."

The original meaning of **octave** was, "eight-day festival".

The Roman year originally began in March–so **October** (Latin *octo*, "eight") was the eighth month.

Something's **odour** is its **reputation** or **estimation**.

Odoriferous means "having an odour or fragrance" while **odorous** refers to something smelly.

An **oenologist** is a "student of wine".

Ogle "to cast amorous glances" comes from Dutch *oog* "eye".

Oikology is housekeeping.

Oil is from Latin *oleum* and that is from Greek *elaion*, "olive oil; other oily substance".

Olfactory comes from Latin *olere*, "to smell," and *facere*, "make".

Olitory means pertaining to or grown in a kitchen garden.

Ombrology is the study of rain.

Omphalophobia is a fear of belly buttons.

Oncology (study and treatment of tumours) is based on Greek *onco-*, "mass".

Oneiric means "pertaining to dreams".

Oneiromancy is dream interpretation.

Onion comes from the Latin word *unio*, "oneness" (*unus* "one") as it consists of a single bulb.

On-line should generally be hyphenated as an adjective or adverb.

Onomatomania is a fear of a particular word.

Ontology is the branch of metaphysics concerned with the nature or essence of being or existence, the opposite of phenomenology (the science of phenomena).

Onymous means "bearing the name of the author" (with the opposite being anonymous) or "having a name".

Opal comes from Sanskrit *upala*, "precious stone".

Opinion comes via Old French from Latin *opinari*, "think".

A cross between an orange and a tangerine is an **ortanique**.

Orthodontics, based on Greek *orthos*, "straight," is the branch of dentistry that aims to straighten crooked teeth.

Orthography is correct or proper spelling.

Orthology is the study of the correct use of words.

Orthopraxy is another way of saying "right practice, right conduct" (**orthodoxy** is "right belief, rightness of beliefs").

Ostrich is from Latin *avis struthio*, "bird **ostrich**," from Greek *strouthos*, "**ostrich** sparrow".

Other is part of a large Germanic word family expressing "alternative".

Outstanding as a noun once meant projection.

Overkill first meant "excessive killing".

The upper lip is the **overlip**.

To **overlook** and to **overshadow** both meant "to bewitch" at one time.

Overt first meant "open, not closed".

Owe first meant "own, possess".

Owl is from a Germanic base imitating the **owl's** call.

Oxymoron (guest host, jumbo shrimp) is from Greek *oxmoron*, a compound formed from *os*, "sharp," and *mors*, "dull".

An unusually shrill voice is **oxyphonic**.

Ozostomia is another word for bad breath.

> **P** descended in a straight forward manner from the 17th letter of the ancient Near Eastern alphabet.

Pacific and **pacify** trace back to Latin *pax*, "peace".

Paddock is from Old English *pearroc*, "enclosure".

A **paean** is a song of praise or thanksgiving or an expression of praise or admiration.

Pair is from Latin *par*, "equal".

Pakistan got its name from the initials of Punjab, Afghanistan, Kashmir plus the ending *-istan*, "place, country".

Pal comes from the gypsy word *prot* or *phral*, "brother".

Palinoia is the compulsive repetition of an act until it is perfect.

Panacea combines *pan-*, "all," and Greek *akos*, "remedy".

Etymologically, **pancreas** (the gland) means "all flesh".

A **panegyric** is a speech of praise, as a eulogy or encomium.

Panmnesia is the belief that every mental impression remains in the memory.

Pants comes from pantaloons—from a sixteenth century Italian comic called Pantalone who wore strange trousers.

Paparazzi (plural) got their name from paparazzo, a fictional freelance photographer in Fellini's 1959 film "La Dolce Vita"; *paparazzo* in Italian *means* "a buzzing insect".

Paracentral is "near the centre".

The beginning of decline or decay is the **paracme**, the stage after one's peak.

Paraffin, coined from Latin *parum affinis*, "(having) little affinity"—resists chemical combination.

Paralipophobia is a fear of having neglected some duty.

Paralysis is from a Greek word meaning "disabled at the side".

Paranoia is from Greek *para*, "irregular," and *noos*, "mind".

Passion first meant the suffering of pain and is from Latin *passionem*, "suffering," as used to describe the sufferings of Jesus Christ.

Parvanimity is "meanness".

Pashmina is derived from a Persian word meaning "woollen".

Pasta is literally "dough" or "paste" in Italian; **paste** first meant "dough" or "pastry".

Pastime is derived from "pass time".

Pathetic first meant "producing an effect on the emotions".

A **pathic** is a passive person or victim.

Pathology literally means "the study of suffering" but is actually used to describe the study of diseases.

Pathos (pronounced PAY-thos) is an English use of a Greek word for "suffering".

Patriarch is from Greek *patria*, "family," and *arkhes*, "ruling".

Pavement is from Latin *pavimentum*, "trodden-down or beaten floor".

Pawn, the chess term, comes from Latin *pedo*, "foot soldier" (from *pes*, "foot").

Pea comes from Greek *pison*, "pulse, pease".

The small wooden ball inside a referee's whistle is called a **pea**.

Peak means "maximize," **peek** means "to peep or snoop," and **pique** means "to excite or irritate".

Peanut takes its name from its resemblance to peas in a pod and has these synonyms: pinda, goober, groundnut, ground pea, earthnut, and monkey nut.

The rough grainy feel of some paper is called **pebble**.

Peck can be slang for "food".

Pecorino cheese is from ewe's milk, as *pecora* is Italian for "sheep".

Cattle and sheep were an ancient medium of barter and exchange—and the word **pecuniary** is from Latin *pecu*, "cattle".

Pediatrician, comes from Greek *pais/paidos*, "child" and *iatros*, "physician".

Pedigerous means "having feet or legs".

Peek first meant "look through a crevice".

Peeve is a back-formation from peevish "perverse, obstinate".

Pelican is probably based on a Greek word for "*ax*"— referring to the shape of its bill.

Pellucid means "allowing the passage of light".

Pen comes from Latin *penna*, "feather".

Pennant is a blend of pendant and pennon.

Pentecost means fiftieth day, as it occurs on the seventh Sunday after Easter.

People comes from Latin populous.

Pepper comes from Sanskrit pippali, "long pepper" **pep** is an abbreviation of **pepper**.

Perdition is the state of complete ruin.

Perfervid is "very fervid"—in other words, glowing.

Perfume derives from Latin fumus, "smoke", literally meaning "through smoke", as the first perfumes were obtained by the combustion of aromatic woods and gums– and their original use was in sacrifices to counteract the smell of burning flesh.

Perimeter comes from *per*, "around", and *metron*, "measure".

Peripatetic itinerant derives from the Greek peripatos, a courtyard for walking about, and **peripateitrikos**, given to walking about.

Periplus is a word for a circuit, tour, or circumnavigation.

Perissology is redundancy or superfluity of words.

A **periphrasis** is a figure of speech expressing the meaning of a word or phrase using a number of words instead of one or a few.

Perk (special privileges, rights) is an abbreviation of perquisite.

Perpendicular was first an adverb meaning "at right angles".

Perseity is the quality or condition of existing independently.

Persuade is the element-*suade* from Latin *suadere*, advise, urge plus the prefix *per*, an intensive.

The root-*turb* means basically "upset", so **perturb** means "thoroughly upset".

Pessimism first meant "worst possible condition or state".

Petrol originaly meant "mineral oil extracted from the ground" and it was not applied to the refined fuel until the nineteenth century; the word came from Latin **petroleum**, "rock oil" (*petr/petra*, rock, and *oleum*, oil).

A **petticoat** is literally French *pety cote*, "small coat", which was originally a tunic or chemise worn by men under a doublet.

Pharaoh in Egyptian meant "great house".

A **phememe** is a name given to the smallest linguistic unit.

Philia is affection or love for friends or fellow human beings.

A **philobiblist** is a book lover.

Philology is a branch of linguistics dealing with changes in language over time and is literally fondness of studying words.

A **philosopher** is literally a "lover of wisdom" *philos*, "loving" and sophos, "wise".

Philosophy is literally love of wisdom.

Natural love or affection is **philostorgy**.

Philter is another word for love potion.

The **phoenix** may get its name from the red flames "in which" the fabulous bird perished, from Greek *phoinix*, purple.

A **phoner** is an interview conducted by telephone, especially for a radio or TV programme.

Phonesthemic words are two or more words that share a speech sound and which have some similar certain meanings, **phonesthesia** (from Greek *phone*, sound + *aesthesis*, "perception") or **sound**.

Phosphorous comes from Grek *phosphoros*, "light-bearing".

Photography is liteally "writing with light".

Phrase first meant "style or manner of expression".

Word selection and arrangement is called **phraseology**.

Pied means "having two or more different colours" and first had the sense "black and white like a magpie".

Pillage is from French *piller*, "plunder".

A **pillowcase** can be called a **pilliver** or a **pillow-bere**.

Pilose means "having soft hair".

A small powerful spotlight is a **pinspot**.

A towing vehicle's rear hook or bolt is the **pintle**.

Pioneer was first used as a military term for an infantryman (French *pionnier*, "foot soldier").

Pious was probably borrowed from Lating *pius*, "dutiful, kind".

Pixel is a blend of pix (pics) and el(ement).

Pizza is literally "pie" in Italian and pizze is a plural of **pizza**.

The material covering of a zipper or fastener is called the **placket**.

A **plaint** is an audible protest.

Plaintiff once meant "person who complains of illness".

Planet comes from Greek *planets*, "wanderer".

Plaque comes from Dutch *plak*, "tablet".

Etymologically, a **plate** is something "flat," from Latin plattus, "flat," and Greek platys, "broad".

Plateau can refer to an ornamented dish or tray for serving food.

A **plinth** is a squared base of a column, pedestal, piece of furniture, etc.

A **plongeur** is a dishwasher, busperson, or other menial worker in a restaurant or hotel.

Plot as in "secret scheme" comes from Old French *Complot*.

Pneumatic is etymologically "of the wind or breath" from Greek *pneuma*, "breath, wind".

A **poem** is etymologically "something created", from Greek *poein*, "create, make", and developed metaphorically via "literary work" to **poem**.

To **poeteeze** is to write poety.

A **pointillist** is a painter who creates separate dots of pure colour instead of mixed pigments; the pronunciation is PWAHN-tuhl-ist.

Polish comes from Latin *polire*, "make smooth and shiny".

Polite actually meant "polished" or "burnished" when it came into English.

Poltroon is a word for a mean-spirited, worthless wretch.

To **polylogize** is to talk excessively.

Poplin may stand for the "Pope's linen".

Popular goes back to Latin *populous*, "people".

Porcelain is from Italian *porcellana*, "cowrie shell", and it led to its being the name for chinaware with comparable translucency and hardness.

Porcupine comes from Latin *porcus*, "pig", and *spina*, "thorn".

Pore comes from a Greek word meaning "passage".

A **portent** is that which portends or foretells something momentous.

A **porter**, from Latin *porta gate*, is one who is in charge of a door or gate.

Portfolio comes from Italian for "carry" and "sheets or leaves of paper".

Post-cenal means after-dinner.

A **potato** is also a hole in a sock through which flesh protrudes.

POTUS is an abbreviation for President of the United States.

Poultry is derived from Latin *pullus*, "young animal" or "chicken"; a **pullet** is a young hen between the ages of chicken and mature fowl.

Potpourri comes from French *pot pourri*, which literally means "rotten pot" and was first a stew made of different kinds of meat.

Pragmatic applies when the question is the planning with respect to these affairs; **practical** is anything that can be done and is worth doing well while **practicable**–worthwhile or not.

Praise first meant "set a price on, attach a value to".

Preach comes from the Latin elements *prae*, "before", and *dicare*, "declare".

A **précis** is a concise or abridged statement, a summary, an abstract.

Precise comes from Latin elements meaning *prae*, "in advance", and *caedere*, "to cut".

Predict (Latin *prae*, pre-, and *dicere*, "say") first was "mention previously in speech or writing".

Pre-empt is from Latin elements meaning in advance and "buy".

Pregnant probably comes from *prae*, "before", and *gnasci*, "be born".

Premiere is "first night" in French.

Premium first meant "prize, reward".

Prerogative comes from Latin *praerogare*, "ask before others", and came to mean "right to precedence, privilege".

Presbycusis (or **prebyacusis**) is loss of hearing as part of the aging process.

Pre-school is the adjective meaning "before school".

President comes from Latin stems meaning "sit before".

Presumptuous means "assuming an unwarranted, unauthorized responsibility".

A **preterist** lives in the past and is constantly nostalgic.

Pribble is vain chatter.

Price comes from Latin *pretium*, "recompense".

Priest and **presbyter** both descend from Greek *presbuteros*, "elder".

In **prime** minister, **prime** means "most important".

Principle means fundamental as in beliefs or truths or understandings and it is always a noun; **Principal** can be a noun or adjective meaning chief or of first importance.

Skin is said to **prinkle** when there is a tingling sensation, as in pins and needles.

Privity is the state of being private or secret.

Prize is a variant of price.

Proactive is the opposite of **reactive**.

Probably should be pronounced PRO-buhblee.

Probate is from Latin *probatum*, "thing proved" and **probate** is the official proving of a will.

A synonym for stormy and tempestuous is **procellous**.

Procrastinate comes from Latin meaning "defer until the morning" from the Latin base *crastinus*", belonging to tomorrow (*cras*, "tomorrow").

Prodigal means recklessly wasteful or extravagant; farmers may make **prodigal** use of their soil and in a pointless war, lives can be lost on a **prodigal** scale.

To **produce** something is etymologically to "lead it forward", from Latin *producere*.

Profer means utter words.

Profess comes from Latin *profitieri*, "declare publicly".

Profession is from Latin *professionem*, at first a "declaration by a person entering a religious order".

Professor is etymologically someone who "makes a public claim" to knowledge in a particular field.

Profile is literally "draw in outline" or "shown by a thread" (*pro* "forth" and *filum* "thread").

Prominent comes from Latin *prominere*, "jut out".

Promulgate is from an analogy drawn by the Romans between "milking" and "bringing into the light of day" from Latin *pro*, "forth, out" and *mulgere*, "milk".

Pronograde is moving on all fours.

Pronoun is from *pro-*, "on behalf of" and nomen, "name".

Pronounce is *pro-*"forth, out", and *nunhare*, "announce".

Proper first meant "inherent, intrinsic".

Property and propriety are doublets, sharing the ancestor Latin *proprietas*, "ownership", a derivative of *proprius*.

The **proscenium** is the part of the theatre space between the curtain or drop-scene and the orchestra, often including the curtain itself.

Prose is from Latin prosa, "straight-forward discourse".

Protect comes from Latin *pro*, "in front, " and *tegere*, "cover".

Protégé is from Latin meaning "protect" and it means "person under protection or patronage of another".

A **proselyte** is etymologically someone who "comes to" a new religion, from Greek *proseluthos*, "person who comes to a place".

Proto-language is any once-spoken language from which daughter languages descend.

A **protreptic** is a pep talk or exhortation; as an adjective, it is another word for "instructive".

Proud comes from Latin *prodesse*, "be good", "be of value".

Proverb, from *pro-*, "forth," and verbum, "word" is a saying put forth as a familiar truth; **Proveriology** is a set of proverbs or proverbs as a field of study.

Provide first meant "foresee", literally, "look ahead" (Latin *pro-* and *videre*).

Psalm comes from Greek *psalmos*, "song sung to harp music".

Psilology is a love of trivial or vacuous talk.

Psychopathy first meant "mental illness".

Psychurgy is mental energy.

To **publish** something is etymologically to "make it public" from Latin *publicare*, "make public".

Puddingtime is another word for dinnertime.

Pugnacious (eager to fight) originated in Latin *pugnus*, "fist".

Punctual (from Latin *punctum*, "point") can mean "pertaining to punctuation" or "of or relating to a point in space".

Pundit is from Sankrit *pandito*, "learned, conversant with or scholar".

Latin *punier* **punish** was derived from *poena* "penalty, punishment" and gave us **punish**.

Purgatory is from Latin *purgatories*, "purifying", and it first meant a place or condition of spiritual cleansing.

Purport is normally applied to things, not people.

A word's **purpose** is its effect, import, or meaning.

Put is one of the most common English verbs, but its origins are uncertain; the golfing term **putt** (from Scottish) is essentially **putt**, just differentiated in spelling and pronunciation.

Pyrology is the science of fire or heat.
Pysmatic is always asking questions.

Q is the only letter not in the name of any state in the United States

Quacksalver, one who quacks "boasts" the virtues of salves and ointments.

Quadrangle is from Latin for "four angles/corners" or "square (thing)".

Quag is a marshy or boggy spot, especially covered with turf that gives way when walked upon–and **quagmire** first meant the same thing.

Quaint first described a peson as being "clever, ingenious" and once meant "elegant, graceful, subtle".

Qualify first meant "to describe (something) in a particular way".

Qualitative refers to the characteristics or properties of quality and **quantitative** refers to the measure of something.

Quality comes from Latin *quails*, "of what sort".

Quandary may come from Latin *quando*, when.

Quarantine comes from Italian *quaranta*, "forty"–the number of days a ship was kept outside port if the ship's people had a contagious disease.

Quarterpace is a staircase landing at which the flights form a right angle.

Quench first meant extinguish a fire or light.

To be **querulous** is to be inclined to complain.

In **quicksand**, **quick** means "alive" as opposed to weight-bearing sand.

Quip originally was a sarcastic or sharp remark or a curious or odd action.

Quirk was first a verb meaning "move jerkily".

Quits in "call it quits" probably comes from a scribe's shortening of the medieval Latin *quittus* discharged".

Quixotic means "visionary" or "naively idealistic".

Quiz has a meaning "eccentric or odd person" and also "a practical joke; hoax".

Quizzism is the practice of questioning or quizzing.

Quoddamodotative is a "thing that exists in a certain way" (or an adjective meaning such).

Quop means "to throb with pain".

QWERTY keyboards are named for the first six letters of the upper keyboard.

> In England, an **R** was formerly used as a mark for rogues

Rabbi means "my master" in Hebrew.

Rabid and **rabies** comes from Latin **rabere**, "be mad".

A **raconteur** or **raconteuse** is a teller of anecdotes, from French *raconter*, relate".

Radiators have a misleading name, as they actually work by convecting heat, not radiating it.

Raj is Hindi for "reign".

Ramification is a subdivision of a complex.

Randy, from Scottish, means "lewd, lecherous" or "coarse, rude".

A bookcase with a double face, as in a library, is a **range**.

Ransack is from Old Norse *rannsaka*, "to search for stolen goods".

The "seam" of the tongue is the **raphe**.

Rapport, from French *rapporter*, "bring back" is based on the notion of "return".

Rare as in steak is an alteration of rear/rere "half-cooked".

Rate comes from Latin *rata*, "calculated, fixed".

Ratio is from Latin, literally "reckoning".

Ratiocinate is a fancy word for "to reason".

Ration is from Latin *ratio*, "calculation, computation," and in the Middle Ages took on the sense of "amount of provisions allotted to a soldier".

Rawky means "foggy, damp, and cold".

To **rax** is to stretch oneself after sleep.

A **ream** used to be 480 sheets of paper and now it is 500.

Rebellion is open resistance to a government or authority; **revolution** is a **rebellion** that succeeds in overthrowing the government and establishing a new one.

To **receive** something is etymologically to "take it back," from Latin *recipere*, "regain".

To **recense** is to review or revise a text; scholarly editorial revision is **recension**.

Recent is from Latin *recens*, "fresh, new".

A recipe collection is a **receptary**.

Recondite "abstruse, obscure" means etymologically "hidden".

Recoup first meant "cut short, interrupt".

Recourse refers to turning to someone or something for help; **resort** is something you turn to after all other options have failed (and as a verb means to have **recourse**).

Recrement is any superfluous or useless part of a substance.

Rectalgia or **proctalgia** is a pain in the behind.

Rectify is based on Latin *rectus*, "right, straight".

Rectigrade describes walking in a straight line.

Redamation is loving in return.

Redeem first meant "buy back" and one of its Latin elements is *emere* "buy".

Reebok is the Dutch name for a speedy South African antelope.

Refer comes from Latin meaning "carry back" and a **referee** is a person to whom a matter or question is "carried back" for a decision.

Refulgent is shining with or reflecting a brilliant light.

Regard is from French *regarder*, "look back at, keep one's eyes on".

Regent is from Latin *regere*, "rule".

Reiki is Japanese for "universal life energy".

A **rein** is etymologically something that "retains".

Relegate can mean "send a person into exile".

Relevant means "worthy of raising in the context of discussion", **pertinent** means "applicable to the point at issue".

Religion comes from a Latin word meaning "reverence" and originally meant a life under monastic vows.

A **reliquary** is a small receptacle for relics.

Relish first meant "odour, scent," then "taste, flavour".

Remark is from an intensified French word *marquer*, "observe, notice," i.e., "making a verbal observation".

Remote is from latin *remotes*, the past participle of *removere*, "remove".

Rendezvous is French for "present yourselves".

A **reprographer** is a person who makes copies of documents.

To **reprove** is to reject or express disapproval of something.

Republic comes from Latin *res*, "affair or thing," and public,.

Repugn means "to strive against" or "be contradictory or inconsistent," giving us **repugnant**.

Require includes the Latin element *quaerere*, "ask, seek".

Responsibility can lie only with people and not with things.

Rest first meant a bed or couch.

Restaurant is a French word taken from the verb *resaturer*, "to restore," and was originally used to mean a food (like soup) that restore; it was first used to mean an eating establishment in Paris in 1763 and in the United States in 1827.

Resteteria was once a term for restroom.

Resume is from French, literally "resumed", taken on anew.

Retrogress is the opposite of progress and it often implies an unexpected or undesirable decline from a higher or more advanced level.

Retardataire means behind the times or characteristic of an earlier period.

Retiracy is another word for retirement.

Retroition, is the action of returning or a re-entrance.

Retrousse refers to a nose turned up at the tip.

Revere is from Latin *vereri*, "hold in awe or fear", plus the intensive *re*.

Review traces back to *revoir*, "see again".

Revise first meant "look again, look back, reflect on".

Revoke first meant "bring back to a belief or a way of life".

Rhathymia is the state of being cheerful and optimistic.

A **ribble** is a wrinkle or furrow.

Ricochet is French meaning "the skipping of a stone on water".

Rickshaw is from Japanese, literally "man power carriage".

Rift figuratively means "to come back unpleasantly to the memory".

Rigmarole may be a colloquial alteration of ragman roll "a catalog, list".

A **rimple** is a ripple or wrinkle.

Risotto means "little rice" in Italian.

Ritzy is derived from the luxurious Ritz hotels.

A **rixatrix** or **termagent** is a quarreling woman.

Roast originally meant "cook before a fire" before it meant "cook in an oven".

Rob goes back to Germanic *roub*, "to break".

Robot derives from Czech *robota*, "forceed labor".

A **robot** is a fully mechanical conscienceless device; an **android** is an autonomous human-like robot.

Rom-com means "romantic comedy".

A long string of beads for prayer is a **rosary**; a short string is a **chaplet**.

Roseate can mean rose-coloured, rosescented, or just plain rosy.

A **rough-rider** breaks in horses.

Ruckus is probably a blend of rumpus and ruction.

Rudiment is from Latin *rudis*, "unlearned, untrained," and is patterned on elementum "element".

A continuous low drumbeat is a **ruffle**, a continuous even drumbeat is a **tattoo**, a continuous loud drumbeat is a **drumroll**.

To **rump** is to snub, give the cold shoulder.

Rainwater not absorbed by the earth is **run-off**.

Rx comes from Latin, with the R standing for "take this" and x for Jupiter, the Roman god of medicine.

S. S in a ship's name stands for "steamship"

Sabbath is from Hebrew shabbath, "rest".

Sabbatical literally means "pertaining to the Sabbath" and "pertaining to every seventh year", an old Hebrew custom Shabath said that every seven years farmers were supposed to give the fields a year's rest, which became the term **sabbatical**.

The adjective "excessively sweet" is **saccharine**.

Safe once referred to a box or cupboard where provisions were kept.

Saga is Old Norse for "narrative".

Saint comes from Latin *sanctus*, "holy".

Salad is a shortened version of Latin *herba salata*, "salted vegetables" (from Latin *sal*, "salt").

Salami is the plural of salame, "salt pork," a derivative of the Italian verb *salare*, "salt".

Salsa is Spanish and Italian for "sauce".

A **salute** is a kiss given in greeting.

A **salver** is a tray or dish on which a drink, letter, calling card, etc. is offered.

Sample is actually an aphetic form of "example".

A **sanctum** is a private room.

Sandal is from Greek *sandalon*, "wooden shoe".

Sane is from Latin *sanus*, "healthy".

Sarcastic means "derisive, tauntingly contemptuous" while **sardonic** means "bitterly scornful, cynically disdainful".

Sardonic is from Greek *sardanios*, "mocking, scornful".

Satchel first referred to a small bag.

Satiate comes from Latin *satis*, "enough".

Satire is from Latin *sature*, "poetic medley," in which things were held to ridicule.

Satisfy comes from a Latin base of *satis*, meaning "enough".

Saucer was originally a small dish on which sauce was served.

Sausage's name goes back to Latin *salsus* "salted" while *wurest* is from Latin *veriere* "roll, turn," a reference to its cylinder shape.

Scalp originally meant "top of the head, cranium".

Scalpel comes from Latin *scalprum*, "chisel".

To **Scamander** is to wander about or meander.

To **scarp** is to slope, cut a steep face.

Scat is slang for whiskey.

Schedule goes back to Greek *skhede*, for "leaf of papyrus," and started out meaning a ticket or brief note.

Schemozzle or **shemozzle** is a muddle or complication.

Sciatic in **sciatic** nerve is from Greek, meaning "relating to the hips, hip joints".

Scibility is the power of knowing.

Science is from Latin *scientia*, "knowledge," (from *scire* "know"), *sciental* is "concerning or having knowledge".

A curved sword is a **scimitar**.

Scissors comes from *cisorium*, "cutting instrument"; **shears** describes a large instrument (over 6 inches of blade) and **scissors** describes a smaller one.

Scold first meant a woman who used coarse language.

The art of writing in the dark is **scoteography**.

Scrabble was originally called "Lexiko" and then "criscrosswords".

A **scrabbler** is someone who plays **scrabble**.

Scrawl may be a combination of "scribble" and "sprawl".

Scribble is a diminutive of Latin **scribere**, "write".

Scribblement is illegible handwriting.

A **scrofulous** person is morally corrupt.

Scroop is the rustle of silk.

Scry is to foretell the future with a crystal ball.

The **scullery**, now a small kitchen, was at frist the department of a household responsible for dishes and utensils (from Latin for "wooden dish or platte") or the room where dishes were washed.

Sculpture is from Latin *sculpere*, "carve, scratch".

Scurrilous is derived from a Latin word meaning "buffoon".

Scurry is an abbreviation of hurry scurry, which was a reduplication of hurry.

Scuzz is probably an abbreviation of "digusting".

Second (as in order) comes from Latin *secundus*, "following".

Serene first pertained to weather, "calm, clean, fair."

Seethe first meant cook a food by boiling or stewing, or to be subjected to this.

Semantic is based on Latin *sema*, "sign, mark" and it means "concerning word meaning," and **semasiology** is a synonym for semantics.

Semaphore is from Greek *sema*, "signal" and *phoros*, "bearing".

Semiology is a synonym for sign language.

Senior is Latin, a comparative form of *senex*, "old".

Sentence once meant "way of thinking; opinion" or "sense, meaning".

Sententious means "full of meaning" and has the same root as "sentence" (Latin *sentential*, "opinion, maxim").

Sentiment is from Latin *sentimentum*, "feeling," from sentire, "feel," and it originally meant "feeling" or "opinion".

Septic comes from Greek *sepein*, "make rotten".

The wall between the nostrils is the **septum** and the bulbous parts of the nostrils are **alae**.

Serious is from Latin *serius*, "grave, serious".

A **serpent** is etymologically a "crawling" animal, from Latin *serpere*, "crawl, creep".

Settee comes from settle but was influenced by "set(y)e down".

Shake is equal to one-hundred-millionth of one second.

The etymological meaning of **shall** is "owe".

Shandygaff is beer mixed with ginger ale; beer mixed with a soft drink is a **shandy**.

Shepherd is a compound of sheep and herd.

Shiraz a red wine, is named for **Shiraz**, Iran, and is an alteration of French *syrah*, from the belief that the vine was brought from Iran by the Crusaders.

Shittle means unstable, inconstant.

Shod means "wearing shoes".

Shore is the general word for an edge of land directly bordering a body of water; **coast** is limited to land along a sea or ocean.

Shruff is refuse of wood or other material.

The bars of a gate are often called **shuttles**.

Sialoquent pertains to someone who is spitting while speaking.

Sibling originally meant "relative," not specifically a brother or sister.

Sibship is a relationship between siblings.

A **siccative** is a substance causing drying, especially when mixed with oil paint, etc.

Sideburns were first called burnsides, named for Civil War general Ambrose Burnside.

Sidewalk's original meaning was "a stroll" and then "a path running parallel to a main one".

A **sight** is a measurement or observation taken with an optical device.

The **sight** is the area enclosed by a picture frame.

Signature is from Latin *signatura*, "sign manual".

Silkworms are not worms; they are caterpillars.

Simmer means "be at a heat just below the boiling point".

Simple means "plain, uncomplicated".

Simplistic means "characterised by a forced, unwarranted simplicity".

Sinister comes from Latin "to the left" – as left was associated with bad omens.

Sipid—of pleasing taste, flavour, or character—is the opposite of **insipid**.

Sir is a short form of **sire**, which originally came from Latin *senior*.

Skinny first meant "pertaining to or affecting the skin".

Skirmish is derived from Italian *scaramuccia* the whirr of birds in flight is **skirr**.

A **skite** is a contemptible person.

Skullduggery is from Scottish *skulduddery*, "unchaste behaviour".

Sky comes from Old Norse *sky* meaning "cloud" and at first referred only to clouds.

Sky-hook means "wishful thinking".

Slacks (as in pants) probably comes from Latin *laxus*, "loose".

Slaughter is from Old Norse meaning "butcher's meat".

Sleek is a variant form of slick.

Sleeveless once meant "paltry, petty, frivolous".

Slickrock is a smooth, slippery rock.

AIDS is called **slim** in central Africa.

Slister is to idle away time, be lazy.

To melt ore and extract metal is to **smelt**.

To **smile** can mean to laugh gently.

A **smilet** is a little **smile**.

A **smockster** is a go-between.

Smog is a blend of smoke and fog.

Smut comes from German *smutzen*, "to smear, stain".

A **snarge** is a total jerk.

Breath going through the nose is **snoach**.

"Snore," **snore** is from a Germanic base imitative of the sound.

Snout and **muzzle** are used for dogs and horses, and include the mouth, nose, jaws.

Snow-blossom is another word for snowflake.

A **snurge** is an obnoxious person.

Dodging an unpleasant duty is **snurging**.

To **snurl** is to turn up one's nose in scorn.

To **snurt** is to expel mucus when sneezing.

Sobriquet is French for literally "a tap under the chin" and means "nickname, epithet" in English.

In the sixteenth-seventeenth century, **soda** was a synonym for headache.

Soda may get its name from Persian "saltwort" or "salt marsh".

Sofa comes from Arabic *soffah*, originally a raised part of the floor made comfortable for sitting with carpets and cushions.

A **sog** is a drowsy state or a doze.

Solicitous can mean "full of anxiety; troubled".

Sophiology is the science of educational activities.

Soporific, "tending to cause sleep," is from Latin *spoor*, "sleep".

Soprano is based on Latin *supra*, "above".

If something is **sorbile**, it is liquid and drinkable.

Sordid can mean "filthy, dirty," physically.

A mute for an instrument is a **sordino**.

The adjective form of shrew is **soricine**.

Getting together with other women is **sororizing** (Latin *soror*, "sister").

A **sot** is a drunkard.

Soufflé, French for "puffed up," comes from Latin *subflare*, "to puff or blow up from below," and also describes types of puffing, like breathing and inflating things with air and a murmuring breathing sound.

Soup is from French *soupe* and maybe Latin *suppa* (from *suppare*, "soak"); **soup** originally denoted a piece of bread soaked in liquid, then broth poured onto bread.

A **sour** is a mixed drink consisting of whisky, brandy, or gin (etc.), lemon or lime juice-hence the name, and sugar.

South seems to come from the Germanic root *sunth/sunthaz*, "sunny".

Sozzled is a word meaning "intoxicated".

Spam, as in email, gets its name from the Monty Python sketch where the word is repeated many times.

Span was originally the distance between the tip of the thumb and tip of the little finger.

Spasm and **spastic** derive from Greek *span*, "draw, pull".

Spay is a shortening of a French word meaning "cut with a sword".

Specialization refers to the process of becoming specialised; **specialty** refers to a special pursuit, occupation, or product.

Specious means "seeming to be correct or logical".

Spellbind is "bind with a spell".

Sphairistike (Greek for "*let's*") was the original name for lawn tennis.

Sphere comes from Greek sphaira, "ball"

A synonym for "to appropriate" is **spheterize**.

A **spinosity** is a rude remark.

Spinster first pertained to a woman who spun cotton, wool, etc., for a living or one who had spun herself a set of body, table, and bed linen—and later was used as a legal designation for an unmarried woman. The activity or product of making fibre into yarn is **spinstry**.

Spissated is a synonym for thickened.

Something's **spissitude** is its density or thickness.

Spite is from French *despit*, "ill will, scorn," from Latin *despicere*, "look down on".

Spizzerinctum is personal drive or motivation.

Splash and spatter are combined into **splatter**.

Splenative is a synonym for irritable.

Splendid is from Latin *splendere*, "shine".

A six-ounce bottle of a beverage, like Champagne, is a **split**.

Spondulicks is slang for "cash, money".

Sponge is from Latin *spongia* and Greek *sphoggos*, "water growth".

Spongeous means "having holes".

A **squadron** is etymologically a "square" and the sense of "military group" comes from an earlier "square formation of troops"; the word was borrowed from Italian squadrone, from Latin *quadrare*, "**square**".

To dirty something through handling is to **squage**.

Squirrel comes from Greek *skiouros*, from *skia*, "shadow," and *oura*, "tail".

Stage derives from Latin *stare*, "stand".

Stagnate comes from Latin stagnum, "pool"; a stagnant pool is a **stagnum**.

In Old English, **stair** meant a whole flight of steps, not a single one.

Stake "post" comes from a Germanic base meaning "pierce, prick".

To **stammer** is to etymologically be "impeded" in speech.

Stampede is from Mexican Spanish *estampida*, "crash, uproar".

A **standee** is a person who is standing.

A husband with marital problems is a **stangster**.

Stasiology is the branch of knowledge dealing with political parties.

Static once meant "the science of weighing," from Greek *statike* (tekhne); the adjective is from Greek *statikos* "causing to stand".

A **station** is etymologically a "standing," hence, a "place for standing," from *Lotion statio* "standing".

The original "**stationers**" or "**stationery**" were booksellers who had a regular "**station**" or **shop** at a university, unlike most booksellers who were itinerant vendors.

Statue, **stature**, **status** are all based on Latin *stare*, "to stand".

Steak seems to be related to Old Norse *steikja*, "roast on a spit," and *stikna*, "be roasted".

A **steam** room is moist air; a **sauna** is dry air.

Steel is carbon and iron.

Stereo comes from Greek *stereos*, "solid," and it was first part of the compound noun **stereometry**.

Stet is Latin for "let it stand," a notation to ignore a correction made to a text.

Stiletto (diminutive of Italian *stilo*, "dogger") was first a short dagger before it was a type of shoe.

Stinko means "extremely drunk".

Stipend comes from Latin elements which translate to "wages" and "to pay".

Stochastic means "random".

Stoke is a back-formation from stoker.

A **stole** is a long or wide fur or scarf worn around a woman's shoulders.

Stool's etymological meaning is "stand," from Germanic.

A **storiette** is a very short story.

Street comes from Latin *strata*, "something laid"; **road** is a general term, whereas **street** is narrower in sense and chiefly urban in application: A **street** typically has buildings on either side and is paved.

One nine-letter word having one vowel is **strengths**.

Strepent and **strepitent** mean "noisy".

Stress is a shortening of distress or may partially be from Old French *esfresse*, "narrowness, oppression," from Latin *sfrictus*, "drawn tight".

Strict comes from Latin *stringere*, "draw tight".

Stridulation is the noise of crickets.

Strift is an act of striving.

The adjective form of owl is **strigine**.

Strike is from Germanic, meaning "touch lightly" —that evolved into the more violent modern sense.

Strong is from Germanic, meaning "severe" or "stiffness, tautness".

A **strop** is a strip of leather used to sharpen a razor.

Studio is from Latin *studium*, "zeal, devotion, eagerness".

To be **stultiloquent** is to be given to foolish talk or babbling;

an instance of speaking foolishiy or foolish babbling is **stultiloquy**.

Stumble is from the Germanic base *stum-/stam-* "check, impede".

Stupendous is from Latin *stupere*, "to be sunned".

Subpoena is literally "under penalty".

The bottom layer of something is the **substratum**.

To **subumber** means "to shelter".

Success first meant "result or outcome," whether good or bad.

Succor is assistance or relief in time of distress.

Succulent is from Latin *succus*, "juice".

Sudoku is a number/logic puzzle consisting of a nine-by-nine grid of squares, each divided into nine three-by-three squares; it originated in New York but the name is Japanese *Su*, "number," and *doku*, "single, unmarried," and was first called "number place puzzle".

Suffocate is from Latin elements meaning "below" and "throat".

Arabic **sultan** meant "ruler," from Aramic *sultana*, "power".

Sultry comes from the obsolete sulter, "swelter".

Sum is from Latin *summus*, "highest".

sumi-e is Japanese for "ink painting".

Sunday is from Latin *Dies Soils*, "Sun's Day".

Sundry can mean "having an existence apart; separate".

Sundae is an alteration of Sunday–either because leftover ice cream was sold on Sunday or the dish was only served on that day.

Supernal means "celestial, heavenly".

Supplosion is stamping the feet in disapproval.

Supply is from Latin *supplere*, "complete, fill up".

Support is from Latin *supportare*, "bring, carry, convey".

Suppose seems to come from Latin *sup ponere*, "put under".

To **surbate** is to tire the feet with excessive walking.

A **surrogate** is etymologically someone who has been "asked" to take the place of another, from Latin *subrogare*, "nominate an alternative candidate".

Sushi in Japanese means "it is sour"; the *su* in *sushi* means "vinegar" and the one ingredient common to all *sushi* is vinegared rice.

Sutile mean's "made by sewing".

Swasivious means "agreeably persuasive".

Swastika means "benediction or well being" and was originally a good-luck sign.

Sweetmeat is made from fruit and **Sweetbread** is made from meat (and is not sweet).

Swerve is related to middle Dutch *swerven*, "to stray".

A **sylloge** is a collection or summary.

Symmetry is formed from *sym-* and *metron*, "measure"—and symmetrical is patterned after geometrical.

Synapse is Greek for "clasp together".

Synergy can mean "the whole is greater than the sum of the parts".

Synesthesia is the commingling of the five senses.

Syngenesophobia is dislike or fear of relatives.

Syndrome is from Greek elements meaning "run together" and is a group of **symptoms**; **Synopsis** literally means "seeing together".

A **synodite** is a travelling companion.

Syringes get their name for the cylindrical shape, from Greek *surigx*, "pipe".

> **T Cushion** is the technical name for the removable cushion in a stuffed chair, which looks like a broad, squat T

The flap of a shoe is the **tab**.

Table tennis is often called by its trademarked name, **Ping-Pong**.

A **tableau** is a graphic or vivid description tablet from Old French *tablete*, a diminutive of Latin *tabula*, "list, plank, **tablet**".

Tacit means "unspoken, silent" or "implied, inferred".

Tachygraphy is the art or practice of quick writing, as shorthand.

Taciturn means habitually untalkative.

Tactic is etymologically "arrangement, setting in order," from Greek *tassein*, "put in order" or "formation" "arrange in battle formation".

Tactical comes from Greek *taktikos/taktos*, "arranged, ordered".

Tactual means "arising from or due to touch" and **tactile** means "capable of, allows for being touched".

Tae-bo is Korean for "leg boxing".

A **tale** is etymologically something that is "told".

Talisman is derived from Greek *telesmon*, "consecrated object".

Contact at a single point is a **tangent**.

Tangible means literally "touchable," from Latin *tangere*, "touch"—it is literally something that can be touched but also can be a feeling so strong that it seems "touchable".

A **tanling** is a person tanned by the sun.

Tapestry is based on French *tapis*, "carpet".

Taratantara is pretentious talk.

The sound of a bugle or trumpet can be called **taratantara**.

Tardy are from Latin *tardus*, "slow".

Tat are worthless articles.

The edge of a handkerchief is the **tat**.

Tax is from Latin *taxare*, "censure, charge, or compute".

Taxi is an abbreviation of taximeter and taxicab.

The fare device in **taxis** is the **taximeter**.

Tazzled is another word for entangled.

A **technolator** is a person unduly worship- fiji of technology and electronic gadgets.

Technology, from Greek *tekhnologia* and its root tekhne, "art or craft," meant "systematic treatment"—as a study of the arts.

Teenful means troublesome or irritating.

Teetotal is total plus "tee" as an emphatic extension (reproducing the first letter)— thereby meaning "total total" (reduplication) in reference to total abstinence, first used to refer to this by Richard Turner in a speech in 1833.

Telephone is from Greek *tele*, "afar," and *phone*, "sound, voice," and it was first called the speaker **telegraph**.

Television literally means "see at a distance".

Tenant comes from Latin *tenere*, "to hold".

Tenderloin is the most tender cut of meat—in beef, from below the short ribs and made up of the psoas muscle.

Tenebrous means gloomy or dark.

Tennis is from French *tenez*, "take, receive," which was originally called out by the server to the opponent.

A **tennist** is one who plays tennis.

Tense is from Latin *tendere*, "stretch".

Tension was first a medical term for the condition of being physically strained.

Tepid is from Latin *tepere*, "be warm".

Terrain was once the exercise training ground for horses at a riding school.

A **terran** is an earth inhabitant.

The word **terrapin** comes from the Algonquin *toarebe* or *turupem*, meaning "little turtle".

The ring on an animal collar for attaching a leash is the **terret**.

A **tete-a-tete** is an S-shaped sofa on "which two people can sit face to face.

Than is ultimately the same word as **then** and the two were used interchangeably until the end of the seventeenth century.

A hollow or rut across a road is colloquially called "**thank-you-ma'am**".

Thin denotes etymologically "stretched"

In Old English, **thing** meant "court, assembly, council".

Thirty, written 30, indicates the end of a story in journalism, first used in Morse Code for its distinctive.

Thousand is an ancient noun originally meaning "several hundreds".

Throne is from Greek *thronos*, "elevated seat".

Thumb was *thuma*, "thick, swollen," in Old English.

Etymologically, **thunder** is "noise," from the Indo-European *ton/tn*, "resound".

Thursday is *Thor's Day*, the Germanic god of thunder (*thunor*).

Tight as in sleep tight may be from the sense "soundly, roundly" of the 1700s.

Timeful is another word for seasonable or timely.

Tinct is a poetic term for "colour" or "colouring matter"; **tint** is an alteration of **tinct**, "to colour".

Titillate is from Latin *titillare*, "to tickle".

A **tittynope** is a small quantity of anything left over.

Tizzy is possibly a blend of tipsy and dizzy.

Tobacco comes from the Carib word *tubaco* which meant the reed pipes in which the natives smoked the dried leaves—but it came to represent the leaves and then the **tobacco** plant.

Toffee is an alteration of **taffy**.

Toggery is clothes collectively.

Togs (clothes) comes from Latin *toga*, from *tegere*, "to cover".

Tonant means "loud, thundering".

A **tondo** is a circular easel painting.

Tooth-music is the sound of chewing.

To **tootle** is to toot continuously, as notes on a wind instrument.

Tootlish is muttering in a childish way.

Top is from Germanic *toppaz*, "tuft of hair on **top** of the head".

Torus, is the cuplike part of a flower from which the floral leaves grow.

To **tousle** is to dishevel or make something untidy; to **tussle** is to scuffle.

Towel once referred to a table napkin.

A group of giraffes is a **tower**.

A **town** was originally a group of dwellings surrounded by a hedge or hill (from German *zaun*, "hedge, enclosure") and first meant "enclosed piece of ground, field".

Tracasserie is a state of annoyance or a petty quarrel.

Trait is a stroke of a pen or pencil.

The fleshy cartilage between your ear and temple is the **tragus** and the downward notch is the **intertragic notch**.

Transistor is a blend of transfer and resistor early on translate meant "transfer".

Translucent is from trons, "*through*," and *lucere*, "to shine".

Trattles are the rounded droppings of animals, rabbits and sheep.

Trauma comes from Greek meaning "a wound".

Travelogue is a combination of **travel** and monologue.

Treen means "made of wood; wooden".

A design of three leaves, petals, or lobes is *trefoil* (as a clover), four is **quatrefoil**, and five is **cinquefoil**.

Tremble is from the base *trem*, "shake".

Tremendous is based on Latin *tremere*, "to tremble".

Triceps means "three-headed".

Trichology is the science of hair.

Triskaidekaphobia is the fear of Friday the 13th.

Trollop "untidy, slovenly woman" may be connected with the word "*troll*".

Trophy once referred to the display of weapons taken from a defeated army (from Greek *trope*, "a rout").

Trouble-mirth is one who spoils another's enjoyment.

The singular of **trousers** is trouse.

To be **truculent** is to be cruel and destructive.

A **trunk** as a box or chest was originally made from a tree trunk.

A bunch of fruit is a **truss**.

Japanese **tsunami** literally means "harbour wave" and can also be called a seismic sea wave.

Tumblers at first were glasses made with a rounded or pointed base so they would not stand upright and had to be emptied in one swig.

A **turtlet** is a baby turtle.

Tussiculation is a hacking cough.

Tussock is a clump of grass.

Tutelary is "acting as a guardian".

Tutor was first a caregiver, custodian, or protector (Latin *tuere*, "look after").

Tutoya means "intimate, affectionate".

Tutti-frutti is Italian for "all fruits".

The **tweeter** is the small speaker for high frequency sounds and the **woofer** is the large low-frequency speaker.

Twenty is etymologically "two tens".

Twilight is the time of two lights, the fading sunset and the emerging light of the moon and stars, and there are three sequential stages of twilight: civil, **twilight**, nautical **twilight** and astronomical **twilight**.

Twitter-light is an old word for twilight.

To **twizzle** is to spin around.

> **U** For many centuries, **U** and **V** were interchangeable, not separated in English dictionaries until c. 1800

Ugly is from Old Norse *uggligr*, "be feared," from *ugga*, "feel or fill with dread".

Ulterior is from a Latin word literally meaning "further, more distant".

Ultramontane means "beyond the mountains".

Ultrasound or **ultrasonography** work on the principle that sound is reflected at different speeds by tissues or substances of different densities.

An **umberment** is a multitude.

Umbilical is from Latin *umbilicus*, "navel".

Umbra is the darkest part of a shadow.

Uncle is from Latin *avunculus*, "mother's brother, maternal uncle".

Underprivileged first meant lacking some legal right(s).

Universe denotes etymologically "turned into one" or "indivisible, whole," from Latin *universus* (*unus*, "one," and *versus/vertere*, "turn").

Unkempt variant of unkembed, from *kemb*, "comb".

Upset first meant "set up; raise, erect".

Upstage in theatre is "towards the rear of the stage" and **downstage** is "towards the audience"; **stage left** and **right** are left and right as the audience views the stage.

Uranium is named for *Ouranos*, ancient sky god of Greek mythology.

Uranomania is the delusion that one is descended from heaven.

Urban is from Latin *urbs*, "city".

Urban refers to a city; **urbane** means polished and smooth, as in a person's demeanour.

Usher was originally a term for a door-keeper.

Usual means etymologically, that which is commonly "used" or employed or commonly obtained—from Latin *usualis*.

Uterus is from Latin *uterus*, "belly, womb".

Utter first meant "outer, outward".

Uxorial is "pertaining to a wife" and **uxorious** is "overly fond of one's wife".

> **V8** is named for its juice content: tomato, celery, carrot, spinach, lettuce, watercress, beet, and parsley

Vacant is from Latin *vacare*, "be empty".

Vacation is a word coming from Latin *vacation*/vacatio, from *vacare*, "to be "free, empty; to be at leisure," and around 1395, this term entered Old English, meaning "rest and freedom from any activity".

A **valetudinarian** is someone who is unnecessarily anxious about their health.

Valid and **value** come from Latin *valere*, "be strong".

Vamoose comes from Spanish *vamos*, "let us go".

Van is a shortening of caravan.

Vanish is from Latin *evanescere*, "die away".

Vanquish comes from Latin *vincere*, "conquer".

Vapour is from Latin *vapour*, "heat, steam".

Vase is Latin *vas*, "vessel".

Vein is from Latin *vena*, "blood vessel".

Velcro gets its name from French *vel(ours) cro(che)* "hooked velvet".

Vend is from Latin *vendere*, "sell".

Sudden or unexpected changes in life are **vicissitudes**.

Victual is from Latin *viciualia*, "provisions" — and is properly pronounced VIH-tuhl.

Vie is a shortened version of *envie*, "make a challenge".

View is etymologically something "seen".

The part you look through on a camera is the **viewfinder**.

To **vilify** is to say defamatory things about someone.

Vincible means conquerable.

Vinegar is from French *vyn egre*, based on Latin *vinum*, "wine," and *acer*, "sour".

Viscerotonic is having a sociable, easy going, comfort-seeking personality.

Visnomy is a person's face or expression, especially as an indication of character and mind.

Vital is from Latin *vitalis* and *vita*, "life".

Vitiate is "to make imperfect; spoil".

Vitreous is from Latin *vitrum*, "glass," and *vitreus*, "clear, transparent".

To **vituperate** is to verbally abuse; **vituperation** implies fluent and sustained abuse.

The adjective form for calf is **vituline**.

Vocabular means "of or pertaining to words".

Voice is from *tin vox*, "voice".

The **voicebox** is the **larynx**.

Void means empty; **devoid** means empty, but empty only after something has been taken away.

A **voluptuary** is one who is totally into luxury and sensual pleasure.

Votal means "associated with or having the nature of a vow".

Voodoo derives from West African *vodu*, "demon".

Vouch originally meant "call as a witness".

Voyeur is French for "one who sees".

Vulgate is accepted everyday speech.

Vulnerable is from Latin *vulnus*, "wound".

To **vum** is to swear or vow.

> The letter **W** is the only letter that does not have just one syllable; it has three

Wabbit means "tired out, exhausted".

Waist is etymologically "girth to which one has grown".

Wan can mean "bland" or "uninterested".

Wane suggests the fading or weakening of something good or impressive.

To **wantonize** is to flirt or dally with.

A **wap** is a piece of string wrapped around something.

A **watermelon** is really a berry and it was first written as two words.

Wax (verb) is from Old English *weaxan*, "to become" or "to grow".

A **waypoint** is a stopping place on a journey.

The **wayside** is the edge of a road.

The original meaning of **wayward** was "turning away" or "turned away"

If one is good at not getting lost, then one is **waywise**.

Weak is from a Germanic base meaning "give way, yield".

Weigh first meant "carry, lift, bear, raise up".

Welcome first referred to a person whose arrival was desirable or pleasing.

Well is an adverb to describe an activity; **good** is an adjective to describe a condition or state.

Wheel is etymologically something that "goes around".

Whelk is a euphemism for pimple.

Another word for trinket is **whim-wham**.

Whisper is from a base which imitated a hissing sound.

Wicked is probably based on Old English *wicca*, "witch".

Wife originally meant simply "woman" but by Old English it was "married woman".

Willy-nilly is a contraction of "will I, nill I".

Wink is the closing of the eyes for sleep.

Workaholic was coined in the late 1960s by Wayne Oates, an American pastoral counselour, from *work* + (*alco*)holic.

To **wrangle** can mean "to scream with passion".

The **wrist** of the foot is the instep or ankle.

All Western Indo-European languages except English derive the verb for "to write" from Latin *scribere*; English **write** comes from a *roo* Wreid, "to cut, sketch an outline".

Wrong originally meant "crooked, twisted, bent".

> In medieval times, most people were illiterate and signed documents with an **X**, which they then kissed to prove sincerity—so **X** became associated with a kiss

X is the horizontal axis and **y** is the vertical.

In mathematics, there are three quantities: **X, Y,** and **Z**.

Xanthodontous is having yellow teeth.

A guidebook for visitors is a **xenagogy**.

Xenodochial means hospitable to strangers.

Xeres is another word for sherry.

X-height is the height of lower-case letters.

The initial letter X in **Xmas** (Christmas) is the Greek letter *chi* of Khristos "Christ".

XXX and **000** added at the end of a letter for kisses and hugs probably originated in the Middle Ages when illiterate people would sign an X for their name and then kiss the paper as a sign of good faith.

> **Y** is the only letter commonly used as both vowel and consonant in English. The vowel is the elder by more than 2,000 years

Year's root sense is "what passes".

Yemeles means "careless, negligent".

In-yan was the Chinese expression for "craving for opium" and **yen** first meant "craving of an addict for a drug"; this became *yan* and, eventually, *yen*, for a "powerful craving".

Yen as in the currency of Japan comes from the Chinese word *yuan*, meaning "round thing" or "dollar".

A **yesterfang** is something that was caught or taken yesterday.

Yestreen is yesterday evening.

Yield first meant "payment".

> For every one-thousand uses of E (the most-used letter), we use Z twenty-two times. Z is the least-used letter in printed English

Zen is from Sanskrit *dhyana*, "meditation" from a Proto-Indo-European root meaning "to observe, see".

Zephyr is a breeze from the west or gentle breeze, based on the ancient Greek name for the west wind.

Zest can be traced back only to French *zeste* "orange or lemon peel".

Zetetic means "asking, questioning".

A **zig** or a **zag** is one leg of a zigzag.

A **ziggurat** is a tower in the form of a terraced pyramid.

Zimbabwe, "walled grave," was formerly Rhodesia.

Ziraleet is a sudden expression of joy, an exultation.

Zoilism is destructive or carping criticism.

Zorro means "fox" in Spanish.

Zwieback means "twice baked," as it is a baked biscuit that is sliced and toasted.

A **zythepsary** is a brewhouse.